Turnaround Principles For Turnaround Principals

Protocols for Creating a Culture of Student Achievement

{Mr. Carr's VIDEO LINKs}

https://youtu.be/3DsoQ_KKlEc (school turnaround)

https://youtu.be/T4bnHKPh6U8 (turnaround principal)

Copyright © 2015 by Kwame A. Carr

(Amazon.com)

All rights reserved. Printed in the United States of America. No part of this book may be reproduced in any manner without written permission, except in the case of brief quotations embedded in critical articles and reviews. For information about the author or this publication, contact kwameacarr@gmail.com or call (404) 247-8517.

Table of Contents 2

Educational Bio   7

Introduction & Acknowledgements   9

Principle 1 – Keep the End in Mind   11

- Cynical…a poem by Kwame A. Carr
- The Best Email I've Ever Received
- Focus Letter to Community Announcing Good News
- Focus Data – 3 Year Cycle – Showing What it Took   14
- Carr's Video: Dept. of Ed. 2015: https://youtu.be/T4bnHKPh6U8
- Parent Email – 1 example out of 1,000 Celebrating Our School

Principle 2 – Things To Do Before the Year Starts   19

- Sneak-a-Peek Directions for Teachers
- Checklist for a Successful Year as a Teacher – Principal Bradley
- Work Rules
- Master Schedule Creation is Priority # 1 – Partial Sample of a Spreadsheet
- Administrative Game Coverage – Partial Sample   24
- School Procedures Protocols
- Staff List Must Be Published
- Opening of School Action Plan Example
- Maintaining from August to May – Assigning Responsibility
- Essential Duties of a Principal   30
- Protocol for Absences
- Preplanning Agenda
- Daily School Schedule
- Sharing Principal Vision on Opening Day - Notes
- Making Decisions and Being Transparent and Moving ON   36
- Assigning Keys
- Afternoon Announcements Form – Create One
- High School Statistics – Knowing the Data
- Welcome Back Letter   38
- Adult Protocols for Positive Environment
- Spelling out the Leave Policy from Board Policy – READ BOARD POLICIES!!!
- Administrative Assignments and Duties – Published   44
- Emergency Coverage Plan for Absent Teachers

- Lesson Plan Template
- New Letterhead for New Leadership
- How to Work in Any Environment – Sample Email Excerpt
- Research on Retention — 50
- Top 10 Assignments for Teachers at End of Year
- Your Day Ends AFTER the Students' Day Ends
- Knowing SWD Data (Special Ed.)
- What Do I Do The First Day of School And Beyond
- Instructional Design – Principal William Bradley Model — 54
- Instructional Strategies
- How to A.C.T. – Administrators, Counselors, Teachers
- Strategies for Standardized Tests — 60
- Curriculum Strategies
- Planning Process and Lesson Design – Principal Bradley Model
- Discipline Process

Principle 3 – Philosophies — 66

- Action Research Findings
- Action Research Reflections
- Carr's Vision, Mission, Value Statements, Philosophy — 69
- How to be a Principal – Baseline Stuff
- Critical Notes for Educators Taken from My Professors — 72
- HOPE Conference Notes 2007 – Marietta, GA

Principle 4 – House Rules — 90

- Leadership Decisions
- Clarifying Announcements
- Changing Bus Routine /Afterschool Dismissal/Regaining Control
- Publishing Bus Numbers
- School Program Protocol
- Miscellaneous Discipline Protocols
- Technology Protocols — 94
- Cafeteria Rules – 30 minutes
- Parents Demanding an Immediate Meeting
- "Go Get a Pass" is not allowed — 96
- Framing Pep Rallies
- Hiring New Teachers and Assigning Responsibility
- Grades and SWD (Special Ed.)

- Preparing Sub Folders in a Red Binder — 99
- Failing Grades Require Parent Contact
- Non-Negotiable Protocols for Everyone
- Grading Policy Design
- Syllabi/Assessments and Grading – Principal Bradley Model
- Laptop Security

Principle 5 – School Improvement — 106

- School Improvement Plan
- Budget Aligned to School Improvement Plan — 120
- Greatest Needs
- Needs Assessment
- Narrative of Needs

Principle 6 – RTI (Response to Intervention – SWD & ELL are mandatory participants) — 128

- RTI Protocol
- RTI Article by Educator David Beall
- Strategies for School Improvement
- Corrective Actions Form — 134
- RTI Letter for Parents
- Sample of Student Identification for RTI
- A Teacher that Led RTI – Dr. Amy Gilbert
- Sample Data – Dr. Amy Gilbert
- Counselor Duties for RTI
- Teacher Reflection of RTI Effectiveness — 140
- Requesting RTI Students during Planning

Principle 7 – Meetings — 142

- College & Career Ready Performance Index Faculty/Leadership Meetings (CCRPI)
- Meeting Sign-In Sheet
- As You Lead Meetings, Realize…
- Sample of Attendance Reporting — 144
- Sample of 6th Grade Reporting
- Sample of Math Reporting
- NO Meetings over One Hour – Parents, Faculty, Teachers, Concerts, Awards, Continuation…

Principle 8 – Professional Learning   146

- Professional Learning Strategies
- Critical Notes for Educators…to Share with Staff
- Hope Conference Notes (2007 – Marietta, GA)
- Feedback to a Principal is Also Professional Learning
- Defining Professional Learning at Your School   150
- Instructional Design IS Professional Learning
- Notes on the Original Karate Kid Movie – Best Professional Learning for Teachers
- Assessment Writing, Technology Integration, Cultural Awareness = BIG 3

Principle 9 – Instructional and Curricular Protocols and Design   154

- Backwards Design Defined as Professional Learning/Collaboration and Instructional Design
- Instructional Frameworks…such as Learning Focused Schools (LFS)
- CDA Protocols (Protocols for Common District Assessments given District-wide)
- Raising the Bar on Special Education : 6-Step Process
- Instructional Protocols - Faculty Meeting Agenda
- Maximizing Instructional Time   161
- Selecting Strategies on Rigor
- Curriculum Strategies

Principle 10 – Discipline   164

- How to A.C.T.
- Discipline Process…Teachers MUST Call Home before Writing a Referral, Barring an Emergency (fighting, physical or sexual assault, cursing the teacher out, etc.)
- PBIS (Positive Behavior Interventions and Supports – Douglas County Schools, GA)
- Dog Sweeps Announced
- Write-Up Form for Adults not Doing Their Contracted Job…Use WHENEVER Needed!
- Calling Student Meetings Frequently

Principle 11 – Interviews   173

- Teacher Interview Prompts (let them do all the talking)
- Counselor Interview Prompts (let them do all the talking)
- Administrative Interview Questions
- Principal Interview – Principal Juanita Nelson   176
- Principal Interview Questions for Future Principals
- Interview with Mr. Carr Conducted by a Mercer University Student

Principle 12 – Sustaining Initiatives on the Inside and the Outside					188

- Writing Across the Curriculum and Referencing Evidence within Text
- Directions for Writing - sample
- More Writing Directions - sample
- Early Payoffs with Writing Honored at State Capitol
- Career Day Phenomenon by Counselor Dukes					191
- Hispanic Heritage Month by Educator Katherine Brown
- Expectations Agreement

Principle 13 – Ending the Year Smoothly & With a Bang!					197

- Afterschool Rules for Students
- Post-Planning Agenda for Teachers
- Teacher Survey Results After My 1st Semester as a Principal (anonymous survey)
- Reiterating Principal Expectations…early on in August!					203
- Olympic Week Tradition – last week of school
- Olympic Activities Described in Detail					207
- End of the Year Checklist Published
- The Last Days of School – Expectations Published					210

Educational Bio

I believe that educators must practice what they preach and provide role models for our children and our communities. In my first three years as a principal, we've turned a dire situation completely around; our students are achieving and our social environment has dramatically improved. Turner Middle School was recognized by the Ga. Department of Education and by Georgia Public Broadcasting (GPB-TV) as an exemplar for middle school turn-around in July 2014.

Education has been my passion for more than two decades. My successes as a mathematics instructor at the middle school level, assistant principal at the middle school level, an instructional math coach at the elementary school level, and as an assistant principal at the high school level, increased my passion exponentially. Throughout my years in education, I've learned a lot as I've implemented teaching standards and set expectations among teachers; and I've seen the possibilities in regards to student achievement. Teaching solely in Title 1 schools has given me the opportunity to challenge not only myself, but my students as well. Through dedication, passion, and research, I've been able develop students beyond the expectations of many.

Understanding the influence of leadership within a school setting has inspired me to a higher calling. In today's global economy, educators must produce students that are capable of sustaining themselves as adults in this technological age. Student capability will come from preparation, which we are entrusted to facilitate as educators. Unfortunately large segments of our student population across the nation have been <u>victims</u> of the "achievement gap." It has been my experience that the achievement gap only exists in the minds of adults. As educators, we are the key factor in student success. Fortunately there are many teachers that consistently overcome all excuses and demonstrate success, regardless of diversity and/or likenesses. As a school leader, it is my job to ensure we have teachers and resources that are benefiting student achievement.

I know that my organizational skills (with an eye for detail), my passion for student achievement, and my leadership capabilities will contribute to the overall success of any school I lead. Being trained in a middle school as a teacher enables me to understand the dynamics of the students and school structure in general. The demographics in my school offer a wonderful mix of opportunities in school support, community involvement and overall success. My school has the potential to raise the bar for all middle schools and to exceed all standards, as measured by the state of Georgia, the College and Career Ready Performance Index (CCRPI) and the newly adopted Common Core Curriculum standards.

Not only do I bring the passion for excellence, but the knowledge and research base as well. My participation as a presenter in local and national educational conferences has sharpened my focus and desire for success, and I refuse to be called a leader of a failing school!

"The 'at-risk' child was born and lives in the minds of adults, not in the minds of children!"

My Education

Douglass High School, Atlanta, GA 1987

Morehouse College, B.A. Economics w/concentration in Mathematics, Atlanta, GA 1992

Mercer University, M.Ed. Leadership, Atlanta, GA 2007

Lincoln Memorial University, Ed.S. Curriculum & Instruction, Cleveland, TN 2011

Introduction & Acknowledgements

The Situation:

I was told that I wasn't ready to be a principal because I didn't know "instruction." Principals don't get fired because they don't know instruction, nor do they get criticized in the public for their knowledge of instruction. They get fired and criticized because they can't manage their entire team; they get fired and criticized because they lack ability to build positive school culture over time; they get fired and criticized because they have money issues, testing issues and/or sex issues.

Instruction can be learned in one month given proper attention. Managing a well-oiled, positive school culture takes longer to accomplish than the time it takes for students to matriculate through your school, unless you come prepared on day one. School culture comes first, not instruction!!! To facilitate an effective, student achievement-driven school culture, you need **protocols**…for EVERYTHING! This is the formula that allowed my school to become one of the top Title 1 middle schools in the state in every category measurable in less than three years.

This book will provide real-life examples of protocols to consider for your school. Many of these protocols were taken from my personal experiences, observing excellent principals and their leadership. I credit these principals: Dr. Lester Butts, Dr. Sam Hill, Dr. Sam Taylor, Mrs. Juanita Nelson, Mr. William Bradley, Mr. James Allen and Mr. Dan Sims. With the knowledge I have gained, my team has been able to outperform most Title 1 middle schools and raise the bar for student achievement by creating a culture of high expectations and a continuous drive for excellence.

The At-Risk Child was Born and Lives in the Minds of Adults, Not in the Minds of Children! – Kwame Carr

Our Demographics:

- Spring 2011 – Lowest performing Title 1 middle school in the district (Needs Improvement Status – State Corrective Action Phase / Focus School – 596 Students)

- Spring 2015 – Highest performing Title 1 middle school in the district and in most districts in the metropolitan area (797 Students – 43% African American, 32% Hispanic, 18% White, 7% remaining = Multi-Racial, Indian, Native American, African or Asian) Free & Reduced Lunch 81%, Students with Disabilities 13% (106 students), English Language Learners - ELL 9% (69 students) – 50% African American Teachers, 49% White Teachers, 1% Hispanic Teachers

The first things you do in the morning, every single morning (and don't let anyone stop you):

1) **Walk the building and say "good morning" to every teacher and staff member every day.** This allows the entire school to see you daily. It also ensures everyone is in place and that your building is safe and sound. Ultimately, it cuts down on morning drama! You'll have to train teachers, office staff, your assistant principals, parents, and community members not to disturb you during this time. I actually got on the intercom and told the entire school, "Please don't stop me in the mornings when I'm saying good morning."

2) **Make the same announcements every morning to students.** This is NOT the time to let students set the tone. **You have a school to turn around!!!** The principal needs to set the tone every single day. Reserve the afternoon announcements for most shout outs or directions, unless you deem otherwise at the moment. Do not neglect to make the same announcement, either way. My announcements go exactly like this:

- **"Welcome back to the best middle school in Georgia. We are Turner Middle School! Students, you have two responsibilities at Turner Middle School. Responsibility number one is to make As and Bs in all of your classes. You have _____ number of days to make that happen this semester. Responsibility number two is to act appropriately, doing those things you learned in kindergarten. For example, young men, you cannot sag your pants, your shirts must be tucked in. Physical and verbal affrays, meaning fighting and arguing, result in suspension from school. Cell phones and electronic devices are not to be seen unless requested by an instructor during their instructional time. You have 3-minutes between classes. Classroom disruptions are not tolerated. You cannot take away from the learning of others. And of course, bullying and picking on others because of likenesses and or differences results in an alternative school placement. Same rules, different day, all week, all year, and forever. At the ringing of the bell, you'll have 3-minutes to reach 1st period. Have a great day!"**

Saying this each morning with absolute fidelity (an AP must say it when you're away) will decrease discipline significantly, reiterate the purpose of school, i.e. student achievement, and put all of the adults on the same page as far as expectations. It's a true culture changer! I've said this relentlessly for a decade from the time I was an assistant principal at another school.

Principle 1 – Keep the End in Mind

Cynical

Everybody living ain't alive,

Just hear me out,

Everybody dead ain't died,

Without a doubt,

Believing what somebody heard,

Or what they said,

Relying on passed down words,

Just use your head,

With billions of people on earth,

Truth twists and turns,

Cynicism questions what it's worth,

The facts we learn,

Do expert answers truly exist,

Each life a tale,

Opinions only guesses in the midst,

You might as well,

Search for the answers for yourself,

How could it be,

Trusting someone's theories being dealt,

Some lame philosophy,

Proven facts change so explain,

Who speaks the truth,

Not promised to be simple or plain,

It's up to you,

To search for the answers and explore,

Does it make sense,

Many make no sense anymore,

And remember this,

Everybody living ain't alive,

Just hear me out,

Everybody dead ain't died,

Without a doubt,

Believing what somebody heard,

Or what they said,

Relying of passed down words,

Please use your head,

With billions of people on earth,

And earth is old,

Cynicism questions what it's worth,

WHAT WERE YOU TOLD?

Written By Kwame Andre Carr (1995)

The Best Email I've Ever Received

-------- Original message --------

From: Gordon Pritz <Gordon.Pritz@douglas.k12.ga.us>

Date:12/17/2014 6:14 PM (GMT-05:00)

To: Pam Nail <Pam.Nail@douglas.k12.ga.us>, Kwame Carr <Kwame.Carr@douglas.k12.ga.us>

Subject: Fwd: Schools Exiting Priority and Focus Schools' Status - Douglas

Great job!

Sent from my iPhone

Begin forwarded message:

From: Melissa Fincher <MFincher@doe.k12.ga.us>
Date: December 17, 2014 at 6:06:19 PM EST
To: "gordon.pritz@douglas.k12.ga.us" <gordon.pritz@douglas.k12.ga.us>
Cc: John Barge <JohnBarge@doe.k12.ga.us>, Matt Cardoza <MCardoza@doe.k12.ga.us>, Barbara Lunsford <BLunsford@doe.k12.ga.us>, "Cowen Harter" <CHarter@doe.k12.ga.us>
Subject: Schools Exiting Priority and Focus Schools' Status - Douglas

Dear Superintendent Pritz

The Georgia Department of Education is pleased to announce schools which have met the Priority and Focus Schools' exit criteria. The following school has met the exit criteria:

District ID	School ID	District Name	School Name	Priority or Focus School
648	2054	Douglas County	Turner Middle School	Focus

Congratulations!

Melissa Fincher, Ph.D.

Deputy Superintendent for Assessment & Accountability

Georgia Department of Education

1554 Twin Towers East

205 Jesse Hill Jr. Drive SE

Atlanta, GA 30334

Focus Letter to Community Announcing Good News

Turner Middle School Excels Academically and Has Been Removed from the Georgia Focus School List Published in December 2011

Wednesday, December 17, 2014

Greetings Turner Community,

Due to our steady academic gains in science, social studies, math, language arts, and reading, the Ga. Department of Education has announced that Turner Middle School is no longer a Focus School. In 2011, Focus Schools were identified in Georgia as the lowest performing 10% of Title 1 schools based upon an achievement gap between two or more subgroups. Once identified, the Focus School designation lasts three years. In that three year period, schools are given support and the opportunity to remove their school from the list at the end of the three years by posting a 25% reduction in the achievement gap. Approximately 156 schools were identified as Focus Schools around the state, and only 20% of all Focus Schools met the goals and will be removed from the list. Turner Middle School outperformed other Focus Schools in the state, making us the model school!

In 2011, our particular deficit was in science and social studies, and the achievement gap existed between our students with disabilities subgroup and our white subgroup. We have closed the achievement gap significantly, to the point where we're actually outperforming the majority of Title 1 middle schools, and some non-Title 1 schools, not only in this district, but in the entire metropolitan area. During the three year period, Turner Middle School has basically improved in every area measurable, including behavior, attendance, course completion, and assessment results.

Our academic gains have been across the board, not only in science and social studies, but also in math, reading, and language arts. **Most importantly, every subgroup has seen significant academic gains in all core content areas.** This means our African Americans, Hispanics, Whites, Indians, Native Americans, Asians, Multi-Racial Students, Socio-economically Disadvantaged Students, English Language Learners (ELL), and Students with Disabilities (SWD) have all made significant academic gains in all core content areas. What we've done in three and a half years is mostly unprecedented! And THAT'S why we're "The Best Middle School in Georgia!"

Let's Celebrate Turner Middle School!!!

Sincerely,

Kwame A. Carr

Kwame A. Carr, Principal

Focus Data – 3 Year Cycle – Showing What it Took

Turner MS, Douglas School District
2011 through 2014

Information taken from the Student Longitudinal Data System.
Does not include summer retakes for any year.
Does not include CRCT-M results.

All Students

Content Area	2011	2012	Change 2011 to 2012	2013	Change 2012 to 2013	2014	Change 2013 to 2014	Change 2011 to 2014
ELA	89.0	94.0	5.0	93.0	-1.0	93.0	0.0	4.0
Math	70.0	76.0	6.0	79.0	3.0	85.0	6.0	15.0
Reading	92.0	96.0	4.0	96.0	0.0	98.0	2.0	6.0
Science	62.0	66.0	4.0	69.0	3.0	74.0	5.0	12.0
Social Studies	53.0	64.0	11.0	72.0	8.0	76.0	4.0	23.0

Black Student Group

Content Area	2011	2012	Change 2011 to 2012	2013	Change 2012 to 2013	2014	Change 2013 to 2014	Change 2011 to 2014
ELA	90.0	94.0	4.0	93.0	-1.0	92.0	-1.0	2.0
Math	65.0	74.0	9.0	77.0	3.0	89.0	12.0	24.0
Reading	92.0	98.0	6.0	95.0	-3.0	98.0	3.0	6.0
Science	56.0	66.0	10.0	72.0	6.0	72.0	0.0	16.0
Social Studies	50.0	65.0	15.0	75.0	10.0	73.0	-2.0	23.0

SWD Subgroup

Content Area	2011	2012	Change 2011 to 2012	2013	Change 2012 to 2013	2014	Change 2013 to 2014	Change 2011 to 2014
ELA	58.0	66.0	8.0	89.0	23.0	84.0	-5.0	26.0
Math	31.0	57.0	26.0	49.0	-8.0	68.0	19.0	37.0
Reading	72.0	80.0	8.0	89.0	9.0	93.0	4.0	21.0
Science	27.0	17.0	-10.0	35.0	18.0	37.0	2.0	10.0
Social Studies	12.0	26.0	14.0	34.0	8.0	44.0	10.0	32.0

ED Subgroup

Content Area	2011	2012	Change 2011 to 2012	2013	Change 2012 to 2013	2014	Change 2013 to 2014	Change 2011 to 2014
ELA	88.0	93.0	5.0	93.0	0.0	93.0	0.0	5.0
Math	68.0	75.0	7.0	79.0	4.0	84.0	5.0	16.0
Reading	91.0	97.0	6.0	96.0	-1.0	97.0	1.0	6.0
Science	59.0	63.0	4.0	69.0	6.0	73.0	4.0	14.0
Social Studies	50.0	62.0	12.0	70.0	8.0	74.0	4.0	24.0

White

Content Area	2011	2012	Change 2011 to 2012	2013	Change 2012 to 2013	2014	Change 2013 to 2014	Change 2011 to 2014
ELA	88.0	94.0	6.0	96.0	2.0	97.0	1.0	9.0
Math	75.0	78.0	3.0	86.0	8.0	89.0	3.0	14.0
Reading	92.0	93.0	1.0	98.0	5.0	98.0	0.0	6.0
Science	67.0	68.0	1.0	79.0	11.0	75.0	-4.0	8.0
Social Studies	65.0	68.0	3.0	79.0	11.0	82.0	3.0	17.0

Hispanic

Content Area	2011	2012	Change 2011 to 2012	2013	Change 2012 to 2013	2014	Change 2013 to 2014	Change 2011 to 2014
ELA	88.0	91.0	3.0	93.0	2.0	94.0	1.0	6.0
Math	72.0	77.0	5.0	79.0	2.0	87.0	8.0	15.0
Reading	92.0	95.0	3.0	98.0	3.0	97.0	-1.0	5.0
Science	63.0	59.0	-4.0	65.0	6.0	75.0	10.0	12.0
Social Studies	45.0	61.0	16.0	67.0	6.0	75.0	8.0	30.0

ELL

Content Area	2011	2012	Change 2011 to 2012	2013	Change 2012 to 2013	2014	Change 2013 to 2014	Change 2011 to 2014
ELA	75.0	59.0	0.0	83.0	24.0	78.0	-5.0	3.0
Math	60.0	41.0	-19.0	46.0	5.0	61.0	15.0	1.0
Reading	82.0	75.0	-7.0	94.0	19.0	86.0	-8.0	4.0
Science	48.0	17.0	-31.0	29.0	12.0	39.0	10.0	-9.0
Social Studies	27.0	4.0	-23.0	22.0	18.0	40.0	18.0	13.0

Mr. Carr's Video from GA Dept. of Ed. 2015:

https://youtu.be/3DsoQ_KKlEc   (school turnaround)

https://youtu.be/T4bnHKPh6U8   (turnaround principal)

From: Gary Wenzel <GWenzel@doe.k12.ga.us>
Sent: Thursday, April 10, 2014 5:28 PM
To: Kwame Carr
Cc: Rhonda Baldwin; Kristy.kueber@mresa.org; Osindele, Lanre; Paulette Richmond; Celeta.Thomas; Melba Fugitt; Amy Cooper (acooper@GPB.org)
Subject: FW: Request to Video Tape (with GPB video crew) you in your school next week about what's working best and other School Improvement topics

To: Kwame Carr, Principal

   Turner Middle School, Douglas County Schools

Kwame,

Our Metro RESA School Improvement Specialists speak highly of the work you have done in your school. We are producing videos of eight School Improvement Modules (Parent Engagement, Turnaround Leaders and Teachers, CCPRI, Indistar, Flexible Learning Programs, GAPSS Process, School Keys, and Leadership Teams). We are interested in coming to your school and filming you, about these topics and your collaboration with the District and with RESA and GaDOE School Improvement.

We would also like to video several students who can talk about what school means to them. And, lastly, I will contact Professional Learning Director Rhonda Baldwin, and ask her if she is available and willing to come and be taped on her role in the district and about the collaboration between the district and the schools. You may have others in mind in your school who may speak to the work.

The challenge is our limited time constraint (who hasn't heard that in education)--we have an open window of next week to complete the on-location filming with Georgia Public Broadcasting. GPB Senior producer Amy Cooper and her film crew are available to film on Thursday or Friday, April 17 or 18 of next week. Monday and Tuesday we are at Meadowcreek High School in Gwinnett, and Wednesday we are at Hartley Elementary School in Bibb County.

First, are you willing to participate? Second, what day will work best? Third, what questions do you have? (See the attachment with history and details.)

Gary

Gary C. Wenzel, Ph.D.

Program Evaluation and Development Specialist

Title I LEA Program Manager

School Performance - Division of School Improvement

Office of Education Support and Improvement

Georgia Department of Education

1870 Twin Towers East

205 Jesse Hill Jr. Drive

Atlanta, GA 30334

Parent Email – 1 example out of 1,000 Celebrating Our School

From: Kay
Sent: Wednesday, September 24, 2014 12:15 PM
To: Kwame Carr
Subject: TMS - The Best Middle School in Georgia - Video on Website

MESSAGE:

Good afternoon, Mr. Carr,

I am the parent of a future student at TMS (she will arrive next year). I watched the TMS video on your website, and wanted to tell you that I appreciate the work you all have done to turn TMS around. I was nervous about our daughter attending, and was thinking about alternatives. However, as I've been "monitoring" TMS's progress, I am actually quite excited about her attending there.

One thing I really appreciate is the approach to discipline, and the high academic expectations you all have set. It's nice to see a school that sees the best in our children (in spite of their backgrounds), and expects the best from them. Young people will rise to the expectations we set for them. Thank you!

You all are doing a phenomenal job, Mr. Carr. Be encouraged!

Sincerely,
Kay

Principle 2 – Things To Do Before the Year Starts

Sneak-a-Peek Directions for Teachers

Monday, August 04, 2014

Turner Middle School Sneak-A-Peek Procedures

5:30 PM Homeroom assignments, bus schedules, athletic requirements/brochures, PTA sign-up, Clubs/Sponsors, counselors, Ed. Evaluator, tag/gifted, etc. in the media center and hallways with an opportunity for parents and students to tour the building

6:00 PM Some parents/students will meet administrative team in gymnasium and others will continue to tour the building

6:30 PM Students/Parents visit Teachers

- Teachers in classrooms, syllabi/course outline distribution, wish lists, supply lists, expectations, parent/student information forms, etc.

7:00 PM Dismissal

1) New students and their parents usually do not know any of the staff or teachers at Turner Middle School; therefore, all teachers and staff must wear name tags, including the principal;

2) As parents enter the school (not the cafeteria), a staff member must greet them and provide them with the procedures and direct them accordingly; **(VOLUNTEER)**

3) The procedures sheet must include the steps for each activity (above) and indicate the completion of the process after the last step. The procedures must include information for 6th graders, indicating where they need to report on Monday morning. **(VOLUNTEER)**

4) Common information like assigned halls, etc… must have signs that are highly visible hanging on the wall which are easy for students and their families to see. Signs placed on tables are not easy to identify and make it even harder to see because of the traffic and congestion in the area. **(VOLUNTEER)**

5) Use a different exit and entrance for students and their families when they have completed a process. Look at traffic patterns and flow. **(VOLUNTEER)**

6) Have staff members with name tags roaming around to be available to parents and students to answer questions. **(VOLUNTEER)**

7) All areas of the building need to be utilized to minimize the crowd congestion. **(VOLUNTEER)**

8) Conceptualize the process prior to the actual event. **(VOLUNTEER ORGANIZER)**

THE PLAN OF ACTION

CHECKLIST FOR A SUCCESSFUL ANNUAL EVALUATION AS A TEACHER AT TURNER MIDDLE SCHOOL

1. Collaborate with teammates; create, support and execute SMART Goals with and for your assigned team and/or grade level;
2. <u>Teach</u> the Georgia/Common Core Standards and their accompanying elements for your assigned subject <u>daily</u> including key concepts from the CRCT descriptors;
3. Use best practice in the delivery of instruction;
4. Complete and submit your lesson plans in the manner prescribed each Monday BEFORE the week the lesson is taught in the box provided;
5. In a conspicuous location in the classroom, **for each lesson**, place the following headings and supporting information under it daily:
    a. **Date/Subject**
    b. **Common Core/GPS or subject standard/Element(s)**
    c. **Essential question(s)/Focus question for the lesson**
    d. **Activating Strategies**
    e. **Instructional strategy/supporting activities**
    f. **Summarizing/Closing Strategy**
    g. **Formative/Summative Assessments**
    h. **Extended Thinking Activity**
    i. **Vocabulary**
6. <u>Manage your students</u> and use the outlined discipline plan at all times
7. Meet your student achievement goals on high stakes assessments;
8. Attend and participate in all meetings relative to subject matter or department;
9. Attend, participate in, and execute, as necessary, all professional learning activities and reach all goals;
10. Collaborate with your colleagues when planning for instruction, including assessments;
11. Arrive to work on time and be in your classroom to receive your students by 8:10 am;
12. Stand at your door and actively move students in the halls to their class with verbal commands at each transition; from 8:10 a.m. until 8:20 a.m. stand at doors moving students into your class;
13. Attend work regularly and follow established protocol to request all leaves;
14. Do not violate the Code of Ethics or the rights of students;
15. Meet all duties and responsibilities outlined in Teacher Keys or Class Keys or any new evaluation program adopted locally or by the District;
16. Follow all established protocols;
17. Communicate with parents and other stakeholders in a timely and appropriate manner concerning all student matters;
18. Meet requirements of your contract and standard teaching practices;
19. Meet your CCRPI goal(s) on the Milestones and Professional Growth Plan Goals;
20. Actively participate in the Response to Intervention (RTI) Process
21. Cooperate with and follow all directives of the administration

WORK RULES - Published

Examples of misconduct under the Work Rules for Classified Employees, which may lead to disciplinary action to include demotion, suspension or termination, are listed below. The list is not intended to include all types of activity which may lead to discipline, but is intended to be suggestive of those types of things which will result in disciplinary action.

1. **Incompetence**
2. **Insubordination**
   a. Insubordination, such as refusal to obey a supervisor's instructions or the use of threatening language to supervisors in connection with instructions.
   b. Leaving assigned workstation without permission.
   c. Refusal to work assigned overtime.
3. **Willful Neglect Of Duties**
   a. Sleeping during working hours.
   b. Wasting time, loafing or taking excessive breaks.
   c. Deliberate or excessive waste of school materials or abuse of school equipment.
4. **Immorality**
   a. Theft or conversion of school property or equipment of a school employee, or theft occurring during working hours.
   b. Possessing, using, selling, or buying an alcoholic beverage, narcotic, hallucinogenic drug, marijuana, barbiturate, amphetamine or other intoxicant or materials represented to be in the aforementioned classifications during working hours or on school premises, or reporting to work under the influence of any of the above.
   c. Gambling during working hours.
   d. Use of profanity.
   e. Possession, use, or display of any firearm or other object during working hours that may be considered a weapon.
   f. Immoral conduct or indecency.
5. **Conviction Of Any Crime Involving Moral Turpitude**
6. **Failure To Comply With All Reasonable Orders, Requests Or Directions Of The Superintendent Or Other Superior Officials**
7. **Violation Of Any Rule Or Regulation Of The Board Of Education**
   a. Use of sick or personal leave for other than reasons stated.
   b. Use of other leave days, i.e., jury duty, military, bereavement, infant care, for other than reasons stated.
   c. Unauthorized absences; absence for one (1) day without authorization or proper reporting can result in termination, but unauthorized absences for three (3) consecutive working days will result in automatic termination. Absences must be reported one hour before the start of the shift.
   d. Failure to promptly report an accident or injury occurring on school property or during working hours.
   e. Picking up or transporting any unauthorized person with a Fulton County Board of Education owned vehicle.

8. **Inciting, Encouraging Or Counseling Students To Violate Any Valid State Law, Municipal Ordinance, Or Policy Or Rule Of The Local Board Of Education.**
9. **Violation Of Any Provision Of The Employment Agreement.**
    a. Falsification of any school record or employment application.
10. **Any Other Good And Sufficient Cause**
    a. Unsatisfactory performance during probationary period.
    b. Any statement, action, or conduct not in the best interest of the school system.
    c. Arrest leading to conviction of traffic violations while operating a school owned vehicle.
    d. Smoking in restricted areas.
    e. Excessive absenteeism or tardiness.
    f. Solicitation for any cause or distribution of written materials or printed matter on school property during working hours other than established breaks or lunch periods.
    g. Faulty or negligent operation of a school vehicle or equipment.
    h. Failure to have a physical ordered by the administration.
    i. To reduce staff due to loss of students or cancellation of programs.
    j. Failure to secure and maintain necessary educational training or licensure.
    k. Deliberate destruction of school property or the property of another school employee.
    l. Fighting or causing physical harm to a student or another school employee during working hours or on school property.
    m. Threatening, intimidating or harassing students or other school employees.
    n. Unauthorized use of school equipment or property.

Employees found to have committed an act of misconduct, which leads to a recommendation of disciplinary action, will have the recommendation reviewed by the Superintendent or his designee.

Master Schedule Creation is Priority # 1 – Partial Sample of a Spreadsheet

Teacher	8:30 – 9:30	9:30 – 10:25	10:25 – 11:20
	1st	2nd	3rd
Kennedy - 6 Math (25)	6th Grade Math	6th Grade Math	Planning
Purcell - 6 Math (29)	6th Grade Math	6th Grade Math	Planning
Kidd - 6 LA (28)	(B) 6th Grd LA CT	(B) 6th Reading CT	Planning
Olorunfemi - 6/7 LA (35)	8th Grd LA	6th Grade Rem LA	Planning
Bulach - 6 LA/SS (32)	(N) 6th Grd LA CT	6th Grade LA	Planning
Davis - 6 RDG (31)	6th Grade RDG	(S) 6th Read 180 CT	Planning
Pitts - 6 SS (30)	6th Grade SS	6th Grade SS	Planning
Tumilty - 6 Sci (24)	6th Grade Sci	6th Grade Sci	Planning
Crumbley - 6/8 Sci (23)	6th Grade Sci	6th Grade Sci	Planning
	1st	2nd	3rd
Smalls - 7 Math (9)	Planning	Planning	7th Grade Math
Smith - 7 Math (15)	Planning	Planning	(M) 7th Grd Math CT
Putman - 7 LA (14)	Planning	Planning	(B) 7th Grade LA CT
Collins - 7 RDG (8)	Planning	Planning	7th Grade RDG
Boyce -7 SS/ELA (12)	Planning	Planning	7th Grade LA
London -7 Sci (11)	Planning	Planning	7th Grade Sci
Norred - Sci/SS (34)	Planning	Planning	7th Grade Sci
Marshall - 7 SS (13)	Planning	Planning	7th Grade SS
Digsby - Rd 180/ESOL (10)		ESOL - 7th	ESOL - 6th
	1st	2nd	3rd
Williams - 8 Math (27)	8th Grade Math	8th Grade Math	**G 8th Grade Math**
Brazil - 8 Math (2)	(M) 8th Grd Math CT	8th Grade Math	8th Grade Math
Lobban - 8 LA (4) CT	6th Grade LA	(N) 8th Grd LA CT	(N) 8th Grd LA CT
Brown - 8 LA (3) Gifted	G 8th ELA	8th Grd LA	8th Grade LA
Mathess - 8 RDG (7)	(S) 8th Read 180 CT	8th Grade RDG	(S) 8th Grade RDG
Gilbert - 8 Sci (33)	8th Grade Sci	8th Grade Sci	8th Grade Sci
Kruzinski - Gifted (1)	8th Grade SS	8th Grade SS	8th Grade SS
Duplessis - 8 SS (5)	8th Grade SS	8th Grade SS	8th Grade SS
Miller - 8 Sci/RDG (LC12)	8th Grade Sci	8th Grade Sci	8th Grade RDG
	1st	2nd	3rd
Sawatski - Gifted (22)	G 6th RDG	**Planning**	G 7th Grade SS
Anderson - FL Sp. (38)	8th Grade Spanish	8th Grade Spanish	6th Grade Spanish
Tabue - FL French (6)	8th Grade French	8th Grade French	**Planning**
	1st	2nd	3rd
Morgan - (17) Office	(B) 8th Grd Math CT	**Planning**	(S) 7th Grd Math CT
Grady - (20)	6th Res ELA	6th Grd Res RDG	**Planning**

Administrative Game Coverage – Partial Sample

AdministratorDuty List 2011-12

Date	Day	Sport	Location	Time	Team	Admin
8.23.11	Tues	Softball	Deerlick Park	4:30	YMS	Fredenburg
8.25.11	Thurs	Softball	Deerlick Park	4:30	CLMS	Rowe
8.27.11	Sat	Football	Home/LSHS	10:00	MAMS	Carr
8.30.11	Tues	Softball	Deerlick Park	4:30	SMS	Rowe
9.01.11	Thurs	Softball	Deerlick Park	4:30	SMS	Rowe
9.03.11	Sat	Football	Home/LSHS	10:00	CHMS	Carr
9.06.11	Tues	Softball	Deerlick Park	4:30	FMS	Rowe
9.08.11	Thurs	Softball	Deerlick Park	4:30	CHMS	Fredenburg
9.10.11	Sat	Football	Home/LSHS	10:00	FMS	Carr
9.13.11	Tues	Softball		4:30	BYE	
9.15.11	Thurs	Softball	Deerlick Park	4:30	FSMS	Fredenburg
9.17.11	Sat	Football	Away/LSHS	10:00	FSMS	Carr
9.20.11	Tues	Softball	Deerlick Park	4:30	MAMS	Rowe
9.22.11	Thurs	Softball		4:30	BYE	
9.24.11	Sat	Football	Home/LSHS	10:00	CLMS	Carr
9.27.11	Tues	Softball	Deerlick Park	4:30	CLMS	Rowe
9.29.11	Thurs	Softball		4:30	BYE	
10.01.11	Sat	Football	Away/DCHS	10:00	SMS	Carr
10.04.11	Tues	Softball	Deerlick Park	4:30	YMS	Rowe

School Protocols

TMS PROCEDURES

1. BUSES – Admin. will only respond to EMERGENCIES during bus duty (7:45 am to 8:30 am & 3:20 pm until the last bus leaves). Please refrain from calling using any means unless it's an absolute emergency. Issues will be addressed during non-bus time. Administrators will initiate and provide necessary bus updates when appropriate.

2. DISCIPLINE/Classroom management - Administration will address major infractions and constant repeat offenders. **The first line of discipline is the teacher.** <u>Make a practice of calling parents prior to involving administration</u>. This usually works very well. Written documentation (by the teacher implementing consequences) is required to assign students ISS/OSS. Just be sure you're contacting parents as your first disciplinary strategy. Use administration to lower the boom when all else has failed.

3. RESTROOMS - If a student is in the restroom without a pass, then they're going to get in trouble...period. It is expected that everyone will assist in this effort, i.e. by signing passes. The exception is in an emergency, such as a student regurgitating.

4. EARRINGS - Boys can wear them according to Douglas County Policy.

5. CURRICULUM - Follow the curriculum according to Douglas County expectations. This is part of teacher duties and responsibilities in Douglas County and in Georgia. Most are GPS driven and are outlined in the scope and sequence provided. Timelines are tight, we know this already. If you need assistance, see me. The GPS link is: http://www.georgiastandards.org/

6. TEAM MEETINGS - Please provide me a day and time of your team meetings. (Grade Level Chairs)

7. CONTENT AREA MEETINGS - Please provide me a day and time of your content meetings. (Department Chairs)

8. CLASS CHANGE (non-connection time) - It's expected that teachers monitor the halls and their classroom during EACH class change by standing in their doorway, no exceptions, every day.

9. CLASS CHANGE (connection time) - Students will be walked to connections daily, by teachers. Upon returning from connections teachers need to devise a plan for monitoring their return as well. This must be implemented no later than Thursday, August 4th, 2011 by each team in the building on a daily basis, regardless of the travel pattern. I will require a brief written summary of your plan at that time.

10. ISS - Students in ISS must be provided assignments by core content teachers on the team.

11. DUTY - Please report on time according to your assignment and the weekly schedule

12. DUTY - If you're a teacher with end of the day planning, then meet administration at the PM buses daily. We know who you are :-)

13. CELL PHONES - These are not permitted at the middle school level. If you confiscate one, give it to administration with the student's name affixed. The parent can retrieve the phone from administration after school only. Teachers are not responsible once the phone is in administrator hands. Don't debate with parents angry about a phone or any other non-educational electronic device. Tell them to see an administrator.

14. **STUDENT HALLWAY TRAVEL** (to lunch, to connections, to assemblies, to restrooms, to the media center) - Travel on the right as an individual and as an entire class. Classes must be in line during these transitions.
15. **INFORMAL/FORMAL OBSERVATIONS** - These will begin very soon.
16. **ADMINISTATIVE WALK-THROUGHS** - These will happen daily, but not necessarily every classroom will be visited on any given day.
17. **INSTRUCTION** - Spend the OVERWHELMING **majority of your time among the students** facilitating and NOT behind a teacher's desk. This is also part of Class Keys which will be used to evaluate teachers during observations. Do your absolute best to teach and instruct from bell to bell.

18. **UNATTENDED CLASSES** - It is not appropriate to leave classes unattended at any time. Students must be supervised.
19. **SAGGING** is not permitted. Please do not condone this behavior by allowing it in your class or in your presence or in the halls or anywhere on our campus during contracted instructional time. The policy prohibiting sagging is clearly stated on the DCS website.
20. **MEETINGS** - Designate at least one meeting per week per content area to collaboratively discuss student achievement data among your team; designate another day each week to collaboratively discuss common assessments (formative and summative) among your team; and designate another day each week to collaboratively share successful strategies - total of 3 days.
21. **LETTERS:** Be sure all communications from TMS or anyone representing TMS are grammatically correct.
22. **TAKING ATTENDANCE:** Be sure you follow all protocols for attendance – i.e. take attendance 1st ten minutes of every class
23. **STAFF ABSENCES:** Be sure you follow all protocols for being absent from work – call Carr.
24. **MONEY** – All money collected from students must be submitted promptly to the office manager; verify the count before submitting
25. **TESTING** – follow all protocols for standardized testing; no cheating; submit tests in a timely fashion immediately after standardized testing has ended
26. **KICKING STUDENTS OUT** – you have the right to temporarily remove a student; however, use your teammates to hold students. Have a plan. Push the office button in emergencies only, using your best professional judgment. We will not practice holding students in the main office. Students must be monitored at all times according to teacher duties and responsibilities
27. **GRADING** – homework will not be assigned more than 5% of students' grades. Summative assessments will account for 50% of a student's grades. The remaining 45% may be assigned by the teacher (classwork, projects, portfolios, etc.). Teachers must update grades regularly and have at least one grade per week. A course syllabus must be constructed and aligned, by subject, accordingly. These will be checked.

Staff List Must Be Published – Sample

Bagby	Attendance Clerk-Health Monitor
Bailey	Lead Custodian
Beall	Special Education Teacher
Boyard	Counselor
Boyce	7th Social Studies Teacher
Brazil	8th Math Teacher
Brown	8th Social Studies
Buchanan	Cafeteria Worker
Camp	PE Teacher
Carr	Principal
Christopher	FLP - Reading Tutor
Cook	Office Manager
Cross	Cafeteria Manager
Crowder	Cafeteria Worker
Cruz	Psychologist - 20%
Davis	6th Reading Teacher
Digsby	ESOL and Reading Teacher
Dukes	Counselor
Duplessis	8th SS Teacher
Ferguson	Chorus Teacher

Opening of School Action Plan Example

TARGET	INDIVIDUAL(S) RESPONSIBLE	INITIAL CONTACT DATE	COMPLETION DATE
Master schedule	**Principal, AP**		
Remediation Schedule in place (student groups identified)	**Principal**		
Critical Incident Response Profile Plan / Safety Plan	**Principal, AP**		
Evacuation Maps (posted in classrooms)	**AP**		
Fire Evacuation Drill Schedule	**AP**		
Fire Alarm Inspection (Bi-annually)	**AP**		
Security Camera(s)	**AP**		
School Mission Statement visibly posted in all classrooms, media center, etc.	**AP**		
Parent/Student Handbook	**Principal**		
Faculty Handbook	**Principal**		
Parent Resource Center (Identified location)	**Principal**		
Registration Procedures in place	**Registrar**		
Opening Day Procedures in place	**Principal**		
Bus Supervision Procedures (Arrival/Dismissal)	**AP**		

Coverage plan for open position(s)
  -Interim teachers
  -Instructional
  -Non-Instructional
	Principal, AP		

Temporary Procedure Packet (lesson plans, class lists, schedule, school map, etc.) and **Form 6037**	**AP**		
Media Center in full operation - first day	**Principal**		
Pull out programs (i.e. ESE, ESOL, Art, Music, Electives	**Principal, AP**		

begin on first day)				
Classrooms Adequately furnished	**Principal, Head Custodian**			
Clean (floors, walls, windows, furniture, high/low dust)	**Principal, Head Custodian**			
Textbooks for all students	**Principal, AP, CST**			
Visually stimulating print rich educational environment	**Principal, AP, CST**			
Classroom libraries	**Media Specialist**			
Intensive reading- Level I and II (secondary only)	NA	NA	NA	NA
Technology visible in classrooms and operable	**Principal, Technician**			
Flag and Clock in every classroom	**Head Custodian**			

Maintaining from August to May – Assigning Responsibility

School Management and Maintenance Plan

Greetings Team,

I depend on each of you as a very vital part to the management of this building, especially in my absence during meetings. I will not miss many days of school otherwise, God willing. As the year progresses, I expect students and teachers to perform and follow all established protocols, as usual, and as displayed these first two days of school (Aug. 4th - Aug. 5th). The only reason things will slip is if we let them slip. The expectations are that:

1. students must report directly to the cafeteria prior to 8:09 AM and sit down, no exceptions, and be monitored by one of you, **especially** in my absence (IB students sit on the stage)
2. students must report directly to homeroom at 8:09 bell and then follow the regular bell schedule
3. the pledge and silent reflection must begin promptly at 8:20 via PA from the front office
4. students must not be in the halls, roaming, put-out, or otherwise, without due cause during class time
5. teachers must be at their assigned duty post during all transitions, including dismissal
6. students and teachers must abide by the lunch protocols of thirty minutes and out, even on taco day
7. teachers must be teaching, not watching videos, not writing a ton of discipline referrals, not locking students out of class, not worrying about book bags

8. dismissal begins promptly at 3:23 PM via PA from the front office, unless bus issues prevent such timing

This student management process will ensure a smooth year and minimize discipline so that we can focus on teachers' teaching and students' learning...

<u>Who's responsible for what in my absence?</u>

#1 Lewis, Merchant, Rowe, Fredenburg - one of you, in that order when the lead is out
#2 Rowe, Fredenburg - in that order when the lead is out
#3 Bagby or an administrative designee - Rowe and Fredenburg - in that order when lead is out
#4 Rowe and Fredenburg
#5 Rowe and Fredenburg
#6 Rowe, Fredenburg, Counselors, Lewis, Merchant - in that order when the lead is out
#7 Rowe and Fredenburg
#8 Rowe, Fredenburg, Merchant, Lewis - in that order when the lead is out

Essential Duties of a Principal

PRIMARY FUNCTION: To build and support an effective professional learning community which promotes excellence in teaching and student achievement. Supervises all personnel serving in assigned school.

REQUIREMENTS:

Educational Level: Masters Degree or higher with a major in educational administration.

Certification/License: SRL-5 in Educational Leadership or eligibility for a PL-5 in Educational Leadership prior to start date with a commitment to earn PL-6 within five years.

Experience: At least three years of successful educational experience. At least three years of successful administrative experience is desired.

Physical Activities: Routine physical activities that are required to fulfill job responsibilities.

Proficient Skills: Leadership and extensive knowledge of curriculum development and elementary school instructional programs. Ability to communicate effectively with others orally and in writing. Ability to budget time and effort. Demonstrates positive attitude toward self-evaluation and self-improvement.

ESSENTIAL DUTIES:

1. Demonstrates regular attendance and is punctual.
2. Facilitates the process for interviewing and recommending new staff members.
3. Leads staff in building and supporting in a professional learning community which promotes excellence in teaching and student achievement.
4. Works collaboratively with instructional and operational staff to ensure that necessary

instructional materials and supplies are secured.
5. Coordinates and conducts meetings with various stakeholder groups to gather input and provide information related to school activities.
6. Maintains physical stamina necessary for leadership role.
7. Maintains emotional stability necessary to perform assigned tasks.
8. Adheres to and enforces state, county, and school policies and procedures as stated by published guidelines and current administrative interpretations.
9. Oversees the financial operation of the school as directed and demonstrates appropriate fiscal management of funds for which he/she is responsible in compliance with all applicable rules and regulations.
10. Demonstrates a willingness to support and implement new educational concepts.
11. Participates in school-related activities.
12. Leads staff in discussion of new materials, teaching techniques, and developments in the profession learned by attending meetings and reading journals or other publications.
13. Handles routine practices effectively and keeps accurate records.
14. Makes the school facility an attractive, pleasant and productive place in which to work and learn.
15. Guards the health and safety of the students in all school situations.
16. Establishes guides for proper student conduct and for maintaining student discipline.
17. Orients newly assigned staff members and assists in their development.
18. Observes classroom teaching practices.
19. Maintains a good working relationship with school and system-level personnel.
20. Encourages teachers and other employees to develop their capabilities by providing them with security and the freedom to do a good job.
21. Evaluates and counsels all staff members regarding their individual and group performance.
22. Deals with students, teachers, and parents in a friendly, firm, fair and consistent manner.
23. Is accessible to students, staff, and community.
24. Establishes and maintains good public relations.
25. Any other duties or responsibilities assigned by the Board of Education.

Protocol for Absences

Greetings All,

Please save my personal cell phone number (below) and print this protocol for future use. Please do not post in a place that will allow student access to my personal cell phone number.

Professional Protocol for Absences at Turner Middle School

(for ALL emergency and unplanned absences…effective immediately)

1. Mrs. Cook is no longer receiving telephone calls, emails, or texts regarding any emergency or unplanned absences
2. ALL emergency <u>calls</u> for sick, bereavement, and unplanned personal leave go to Mr. Carr <u>only,</u> via phone
3. Please know and understand the reasons that I do not accept text messages or emails; if you have questions, please see me personally
4. <u>ALL Emergency and Unplanned absences must be phoned in</u> to Mr. Carr **@ XXX XXX XXXX** (**not** my office phone at TMS)
    a. After hours you may call up until 10 PM (M-F)
    b. No calls on Saturdays (that's my family day…no exceptions please)
    c. Sundays you may call between 12 noon and 10 PM
5. Please do NOT call Mr. Carr before 5:30 AM (M-F) or after 7 AM (M-F)
6. We must have adequate time to prepare for any unexpected, unplanned, emergency absences, and this is just good old <u>professionalism in practice</u>
7. If you're already at work and need to leave, then seek an assistant principal for coverage first. If your emergency requires the next day off, then follow the aforementioned protocol, i.e. <u>call me</u>
8. Legal leave, jury duty leave, professional duty leave, adoption leave, military leave, family medical leave are known in advance and must be reported according to DCS policy (below)
9. SUMMARY of Protocol for all <u>unplanned sick</u>, <u>emergency personal</u>, <u>unexpected bereavement</u> absences:

    - **<u>Call Mr. Carr</u> up until 10 PM (M - F)**
    - **OR <u>Call Mr. Carr</u> between 5:30 AM - 7:00 AM (M – F)**
    - **OR <u>Call Mr. Carr</u> Sundays 12 – 10 PM**

10. Please do not violate this protocol by calling, texting, or emailing absences to Mrs. Cook or anyone else. <u>Mr. Carr receives all emergency calls</u>…if no answer, then please leave a detailed professional message indicating your name, number, and reason for absence within the given timeframes stipulated above

Preplanning Agenda

Monday, August 1, 2011

07:30 - 08:15	Breakfast Served/Key Distribution
08:15 - 10:10	Principal's Vision - meet with all staff
10:10 - 10:25	Break
10:30 - 12:00	SIS Training for Teachers in TMS Media Center
12:00 - 01:00	Lunch on your own
01:00 - 03:30	Department – Grade Level Meetings/Work in Rooms
03:30 - 08:00	Building Open

Tuesday, August 2, 2011

08:00 - 03:30	System-wide Professional Development Day
08:00 - 03:59	Building Open/Work in Rooms/Lunch on your own
04:00 - 06:00	Sneak-A-Peek begins in cafeteria (see agenda)
06:00 - 08:00	Building Open

Wednesday, August 3, 2011

08:00 - 10:00	Coaches' Meeting with A.D./Work in rooms
10:00 - 11:00	Faculty Meeting (cafeteria) Books/Schedules/Discipline
11:00 - 12:00	Lunch – on your own
12:00 - 02:00	Master Calendar/Safety/Subs/Duties/1st day procedures
02:00 - 02:15	Break
02:20 - 03:30	Tie up loose ends – Faculty Meeting in the Cafeteria
03:30 - 08:00	Building Open

Thursday, August 4, 2011

FIRST DAY OF SCHOOL!!!!!!!!!!!!!!!!!!!!!!!!!!!!! *The building will be open until 11:00pm every evening this week.*

Daily School Schedule

2011 – 2012

08:10 Teachers must have repor<u>ted</u> to their classroom doorway or assigned duty, daily

08:09 Student dismissal from cafeteria – Students report to homeroom

08:10 – 08:27 Homeroom

08:30 – Tardy (students w/ parents check in at main office to receive tardy pass)

08:30 – 9:20   1st period   <u>50 minutes</u>   (7th grade planning/connections)

09:23 – 10:13 2nd period   <u>50 minutes</u>   (7th grade planning/connections)

10:16 – 11:06 3rd period   <u>50 minutes</u>   (6th grade planning/connections)

11:09 – 12:50 4th period   (planning for connections)

- 11:14 – 11:44 =   6th grade lunch   (30 minutes)
- 11:47 – 12:17 =   7th grade lunch   (30 minutes)
- 12:20 – 12:50 =   8th grade lunch   (30 minutes)

12:53 – 01:43 5th period   <u>50 minutes</u>   (6th grade planning/connections)

01:46 – 02:36 6th period   <u>50 minutes</u>   (8th grade planning/connections)

02:39 – 03:30 7th period   <u>51 minutes</u>   (8th grade planning/connections)

03:30-ish Teachers dismiss students at announcement ONLY and fulfill remaining duties until allowable departure time

Straight Traditional Schedule, i.e. no T.M.S. week designations and <u>no rotating weeks</u>

<u>Connections</u> classes last 9 weeks, then connections' schedules change

<u>Teachers without homerooms have morning duty beginning at 8:10 AM</u>

<u>8th grade</u> teachers have <u>afternoon duty</u> at buses or hallway duty during dismissal, daily

Mr. Rowe assigns all duties; please report accordingly

Sharing Principal Vision on Opening Day 2013 – Notes

Video (Say It Long Enough and It Becomes a Part of You)
Professional Learning this summer / who learned/what's new?
Think Like a Patron book summary –**TEACHERS** are the key, not the principal, supt., board members
Rising Expectations & Vision for Each Staff Member

Changes:
1. Writing plan for teachers - 5 assignments, papers with commentary, no lesson plans for a month, ELA review during planning, teachers choose topic
2. RTI plan
3. 4 lunches
4. ELA Leadership/8th Grade Leadership Changes

Resolve issues with paperwork in special ed and counseling

Focus Team Meeting Objectives will be aligned to all meetings:

1. Productive and Efficient, Purposeful, Time Conscious
2. Agenda is Data-Driven
3. Student Focused
4. Everyone's Voice is Heard, Atmosphere of Collegiality, Build Consensus, Use Protocols

CURRICULUM (standards), INSTRUCTION (Learning Focused Schools), ASSESSMENT (Balanced)

DCSS Academic Focus = what we teach; How we teach; How we assess

Great Behavior + Great Teaching = Great Achievement/Grades

"If it matters to you, you will find a way. If it doesn't, you will find an excuse." Unknown Author

"Don't make excuses; you signed up for this!" Carr

GOALS

Increases in Writing, Reading, ELA, Math, Science, Social Studies – As & Bs for TEACHERS

Authentic Lessons have: Academic Language –

1. Reading, Writing, Speaking, Thinking the Language IN Class

Promote school-wide reading for fun; Use articles geared towards students

Turn-around Leaders/Teachers have a pattern of thinking, feeling, acting, speaking: (publicimpact.com)

1. Drive for results
2. Influencing for results (positive)
3. Problem solving, not whining about problems
4. Showing confidence to lead/teach

Making Decisions and Being Transparent and Moving ON – Sample Communication

From: Kwame Carr
Sent: Wednesday, August 07, 2013 1:11 PM
To: Jones
Cc: Turner Middle
Subject: (UPDATE requested 8/7/13) Bell Schedule w 4 Lunches

Greetings Mr. Jones,

After observing the **traffic patterns the first day of school**, it is obvious we need to adjust lunch as our population grows. This is my last time requesting a bell schedule change - I promise. Please tweak the bells according to the highlighted times only. My apologies to those grade levels that have posted their schedules or perhaps had them blown up and laminated. Mrs. Fredenburg, please send the updated times to C.O. as well once they're installed.

Lastly, I left you a voicemail, Mr. Jones. When you get a moment, please let me know when the new bells will be in effect.

Thank you for everything!
K.Carr

Assigning Keys - Sample

SCHOOL NAME ___Turner Middle School_____

Employee	Title	Key #	Which will Open
Patrick	Teacher	1D61	17
Kim	Counselor	1DM,1DY11D2	Rm 26, Master
Rodney	Teacher	1DM,1050	Rm 5, athletic
Theresa	Teacher	1D27,Rm 303	Rm 38
Sherrie	Teacher	1D23	Rm 27
Roxanne	Teacher	1D28, 138	Rm 29, desk
Angela	Teacher	1033	Rm 24, cabinets & storage
Jaslyn	Counselor	1DM	Rm 18, Master
Alicia	Counselor	1D2	Rm of mailroom
Jamie	Teacher	1D24, 1D61	Rm 25, concessions
Tom	Teacher	1D46,1D60,61	Rm 21, athletic storage
Jessica	Teacher	1D55	Rm22
Barbara	Title one	1D1Y	Trailer

Afternoon Announcements Form – Create One

From: Ryan
Sent: Monday, October 7, 2013 12:06 PM
To: Turner Middle
Subject: Afternoon Announcements

Best Teachers in the Best Middle School In GA,

As we move further in the year and the announcement folder fills we need to facilitate a quicker end of day procedure. Attached you will find a form for all announcements to be given.

Starting after fall break, <u>this form must be in the folder for any announcement to be made</u>. If you currently have an announcement in the folder, please discard it and use the attached form. The only exception to the use of this form is office personnel.

High School Statistics – Knowing the Data

http://www.graduatefirstfundamentals.org

WHAT THE LATEST RESEARCH SHOWS

Long range goal is for our students to graduate from high school by providing opportunities in elementary and middle grades, which can prevent them from dropping out of school.

Decrease gaps between SWD and all students in the areas of attendance, ISS, OSS, and achievement.

- **Predictors of Dropout**
    1. The four strongest predictors – determined by the end of sixth grade
        1. Poor attendance *(14% graduated on time or with one extra year)*
        2. Poor behavior *(17% on-time graduation rate)*
        3. Failing math *(21% on-time graduation rate)*
        4. Failing English *(16% on-time graduation rate*
    2. Sixth graders who do not attend school regularly, receive poor behavior marks, or fail math or English
    3. <u>Students who repeated middle school grades are **11** times more likely to drop out than students who had not repeated</u>
    4. A student who is retained two grades increases their risk of dropping out of school by 90%
    5. Transitions between schools
- Signs of Disengagement
    - Low motivation – dislike of school
    - Low rates of responding in class

- Absenteeism – absent >10 days per year
- Poor academic performance – failed 3-5 classes
- Grade retention – retained one or more years
- Behavior issues – 5 disciplinary referrals
- Little or no participation in school activities
- Intervention Basics:
    - Target list of students (50-52 at-risk; at least ½ SWD; others still need to be at-risk based on absenteeism, behavior, course performance and other factors which may include Milestones scores and grade retention)
    - Data Collection – 1) Attendance, ISS, OSS, Course failures - 4 x a year; 2) Data Probe
    - Bi-monthly Team Leader Meetings (Attendees may include Team Leader, Principal, Assistant Principal, other member of Focus Team)
    - Means of informing and including faculty in Focus activities and initiatives **(CCRPI Meetings)**

Welcome Back Letter

From: Kwame Carr
Sent: Tuesday, July 15, 2014 2:22 PM
To: Turner Middle
Subject: Welcome Back to Turner Middle School 2014 - 2015

Greetings Turner! (Don't read until July 29th if you're not in the mood :-)

As we begin a new school year, my hope is that you've found time to rest, relax, and rejuvenate. If not, then please do your best to take these last two weeks to do something for yourself in that regard! My "summer" flew by but I'm ready to go into another year fully charged. Our goal for the upcoming year is simple - Be Better! On a personal level, that means that I've dedicated this summer and the rest of my living days to becoming spiritually, mentally, and physically better than when we last saw each other. In doing so, my goal of being professionally better can only be enhanced and more achievable. I hope you will join me with the same positive attitude by continually taking positive actions towards the betterment of yourselves, our students, and Turner Middle School.

The foundation we've set is set in stone, as we've seen student achievement significantly rise for three consecutive years. Even with the new assessment changes (Milestones) and the new teacher evaluation system (Teacher Keys), we will succeed and be competitive in Douglas County, Georgia, and the nation. **The data we've amassed speaks for itself!** No words needed... Anything less than continuing to offer a competitive education for our students is not up for discussion; we already know the expectations at Turner, for Turner. With these thoughts and expectations in mind, please enjoy your remaining time away, and prepare holistically for another fantastic year at "the best middle school in Georgia!" We bid farewell to the staff that have served us well over the past years and welcome the new staff for the upcoming year. Every single addition to our staff this year is PHENOMENAL!

Adult Protocols for Positive Environment

From: Kwame Carr
Sent: Monday, September 22, 2014 5:03 PM
To: Turner Middle
Subject: Adult Protocol for Maintaining a Positive Spirit @ TMS

Being positive at TMS is totally a choice, especially among **adults**, because <u>we choose to be here</u> to promote the positive or the negative at any given moment. At Turner, we welcome and embrace positivity, and our goal is to maximize it! To accomplish our goal, it is necessary to minimize and do our best to eliminate negativity. ***Research has clearly shown the impact of ingrained beliefs on our outer experiences in life.*** We are what we constantly think about, say, and act upon, and our life experiences follow.

"Adults have two responsibilities at Turner Middle School."

1. **Create a safe, secure, and effective learning environment for students to make As and Bs**
2. **Act Appropriately, which we will define by the following:**

    - Work cooperatively and collaboratively with all adults for the betterment of our students at all times
    - Uphold all duties and responsibilities as outlined in our job descriptions and by TMS protocols
    - No bad mouthing our colleagues/co-workers - if there's an issue, see an administrator or resolve it yourselves as adults
    - Abstain from rumor, hearsay, and/or any action or attitude that is deleterious to the collegial/familial environment we've created at TMS

For Absolute Clarity - Please remember this as we go forward. Adults failing to meet these 2 basic responsibilities fail to meet them <u>by choice</u>.

Kwame A. Carr

Principal

Turner Middle School

| **Spelling out the Leave Policy from Board Policy – READ BOARD POLICIES!!!!!** |

SICK LEAVE

All benefits-eligible personnel employed by the School System shall be eligible for sick leave earned at the rate of one and one-fourth days for each school month worked, provided salary is earned for at least half of the work days in the month. Sick leave is not earned while the employee is on leave without pay or when an employee is on leave using days awarded by the Sick Leave Bank. Any unused sick leave may be carried forward from one fiscal year to the next. A credit of no more than the maximum amount of sick leave to be earned during the school year is credited in advance to each employee paid on a monthly basis at the beginning of their contract year. In the event of separation of service, deductions in amounts sufficient to cover the sick leave not earned by said employee shall be made from said employee's regular salary which may be due. If there are insufficient funds in the employee's remaining pay, the employee will be responsible for reimbursing the Board of Education.

Eligibility for sick leave shall be based on the following:

1. Personal illness;
2. Incapacity because of bodily injury;
3. Exposure to contagious disease by which the health of the pupils would be endangered by attendance on duty;
4. Illness in immediate family which necessitates continuing supervision and care of employee. Immediate family shall include husband, wife, father, mother, brother, sister, son, daughter, or a person standing in loco parentis. Any days missed because of illness of any person other than on the list above must be taken from personal leave;
5. Sick leave may be utilized for absence due to physical disability related to pregnancy or childbirth. However, if the local School Board disagrees with any doctor's statement of disability or ability, it may appoint a physician of the same medical specialty as the employee's physician for the purpose of receiving independent medical judgment. If not eligible for Family Medical Leave, only one employee in a family shall be granted a pregnancy or childbirth leave of absence.
6. Bereavement (Death)
7. Adoption/Foster Child Placement
8. Personal Leave

<u>A doctor's certificate may be required by the Superintendent or designee at any time deemed necessary</u>, but shall be required for any illness longer than three (3) consecutive days. A doctor's certificate will be required in most instances however, should extenuating circumstances occur where a doctors certificate is not available, **the employees should contact the principal of the building who should then report to the appropriate Superintendent's designee who may waive the requirement for any days missed if sick leave is granted at the beginning or end of the school year, teacher work days, parent conference days, in-service days, or the day before or day after a holiday period (first day before and/or first day after).**

Central Office employees should report extenuating circumstances to their appropriate supervisor, who shall then report to the Superintendent's designee, who may waive the requirement.

For any absence an employee shall file a leave form in the office of the principal/supervisor giving dates and reasons for absence. For absences beyond the three (3) days, a doctor's certificate or its equivalent shall be filed with the statement of absence. One copy of the form and the doctor's certificate shall be kept on file by the principal/supervisor.

An employee knowing of a future confinement shall notify the immediate supervisor in writing as soon as it is medically determined by a physician, the anticipated date of confinement and the approximate date the employee can return to the assigned duties. A doctor's statement must accompany the employee's statement. This is necessary in order to avoid any misunderstandings in the employment of the substitute or the employment of a replacement.

After having exhausted accumulated sick leave, Family Medical Leave (if eligible), and all other leave and being off payroll for a period of thirty (30) days, the position shall be declared vacant. The thirty (30) day period of being off payroll can include the time that an employee is on Family Medical Leave, if all other leave is exhausted. Following such a termination and after having received a statement from the doctor indicating physical and mental fitness for re-employment, a written request for re-employment may be submitted to the Director of Human Resources. Consideration will be given over new applicants, as vacancies within areas of preparation occur.

An employee of the local board of education may donate up to ten sick leave days to his or her spouse if such spouse is also an employee of the local board for purposes of maternity leave, illness, illness of a family member, or death of a family member. The ten additional sick days may be used only after the entire employee's accumulated days are exhausted.

EXTENDED LEAVE

Extended leave is defined as any qualified sick leave which extends beyond ten (10) working days. A Request for Family and Medical Leave/Extended Leave must be completed and submitted to the Human Resource Department.

PERSONAL LEAVE

Personal leave will be limited to three (3) days per school year and will be deducted from the employee's accumulated sick leave. Personal leave will be granted dependent on assurance that the employee's responsibilities will be covered. Request for such leave shall be made in writing (Leave Form) to the employee's immediate supervisor or designee.

Personal leave cannot be taken at the beginning of the school year, on teacher work days, parent conference days, in-service days, on the day before or after a holiday except in extreme emergencies and with special approval of the Superintendent or designee. No carry-over of personal days will be allowed from one year to the next. Unused personal leave will be carried over as accumulated sick leave.

PROFESSIONAL LEAVE

Professional leave may be granted during the employee work day to permit the certified or classified employee to serve as an officer or attend conferences and conventions of recognized professional organizations. Professional leave may also be granted for short term in-service, workshop, or planning meetings dealing with the system-wide program. Request for such leave shall be made in writing (Leave Form) and granted in advance (prior to conference registration) to the employee's immediate supervisor or designee. Each request shall be considered on its merit and shall include a plan for carrying out the duties of the employee while on professional leave. Approval/disapproval of professional leave will be made in writing (Leave Form) from the immediate supervisor or designee.

BEREAVEMENT (DEATH) LEAVE

Death in Immediate Family

In the event of a death in the immediate family of a benefits-eligible employee, a leave-of-absence of no more than three sick leave days will be granted for the death of an immediate family member in state and up to five days for the death of an immediate family member out of state. Any absence due to the death of a person other than on the list below must be taken from personal leave.

For the purpose of this policy provision, immediate family members are defined as: husband, wife, father, mother, son, daughter, brother, sister, father-in-law, mother-in-law, brother-in-law, sister-in-law, daughter-in-law, son-in-law, granddaughter, grandson, grandfather, grandmother, aunt, uncle, niece, nephew, and any relatives living in the immediate household of the employee.

Exceptions to the above must be approved by the Superintendent or designee.

Request for such leave shall be made in writing (Leave Form) to the employee's immediate supervisor or designee.

ADOPTION/FOSTER CHILD PLACEMENT LEAVE

An adoption leave of absence shall be granted to employees of the Board of Education in accordance with the following guidelines:

1. Notice. Except where circumstances are such that reasonable advance planning is not possible, employees must provide the immediate supervisor and the Douglas County School System Central Office with not less than 30 days' notice before the date the leave is to begin, except that if the date of placement requires leave to begin is less than 30 days, the employee shall provide such notice as is practicable. The employee must complete a Request for Family and Medical Leave/Extended Leave Form (GBRIG-E1/GCRGG-E1). Certification from the agency or the attorney through which the child is to be adopted shall be included in the application.
2. Extent of Leave. If an employee is not eligible for Family Medical Leave, the employee may use up to 30 days accumulated sick leave for adoption leave, or adoption leave without pay may be granted if the employee desires.
3. Commencement. When the employee is notified that a child is available, the employee will immediately notify the supervisor or principal. A conference will be held to determine specific adoption leave dates for commencement and return to work.
4. Return to Work. An employee who has been granted adoption leave for a period of 30 days or less shall be entitled to active employment at the end of such period of leave and shall be assigned to a substantially equivalent position to be approved by the Superintendent. An employee who does not return to work in accordance with the above, without receiving approval for a change in the adoption leave status from the Superintendent and/or Board, shall be deemed to have voluntarily terminated employment. Such an employee may re-apply and be considered for any vacant position of which they apply.
5. Limitations. An employee who has acquired a step child/step children as a result of a marriage and who seeks to adopt the step child/step children shall not be eligible for an adoption leave of absence.
If not eligible for Family Medical Leave, only one employee in a family shall be granted an adoption leave of absence.

LEGAL LEAVE

Douglas County school employees are entitled to time off to vote in any municipal, county, State, or federal election or primary without loss of pay or benefits, not to exceed two hours, but if the employee's work begins at least two hours after the polls open or ends at least two hours before the polls close, this law does not apply. Time off must be approved by the immediate supervisor or designee.

There shall be no loss of pay or benefits because of jury duty absence nor shall such employee utilizing jury leave be required to pay cost of employing a substitute. Employees may retain all jury duty pay. Request for such leave shall be made in writing (Leave Form) to the employee's immediate supervisor or designee. A copy of the jury summons should be attached to the request for leave.

There shall be no loss of pay or benefits to an employee who is absent from employment for the purpose of attending judicial proceedings in response to a subpoena, or other court order or process which requires the attendance of the employee at the judicial proceedings. Request for such leave shall be made in writing (Leave Form) to the employee's immediate supervisor or designee. A copy of the subpoena or court order should be attached to the request for leave.

MILITARY LEAVE

All persons employed in any capacity in the school system (other than those employed on a temporary basis) shall be entitled to military leave for ordered military duty with full employment and reinstatement rights as provided by law. An employee shall be allowed a leave of absence from the duties while performing ordered military duty. Request for such leave shall be made in writing (Leave Form) to the employee's immediate supervisor or designee. A copy of the military orders should be attached to the request for leave.

Definition

The term ordered military duty as defined by O.C.G.A. § 38-2-279, shall mean the following:

Any military duty performed in the service of the State or of the United States, including, but not limited to, attendance at any service school or schools conducted by the armed forces of the United States by an employee as a voluntary member of any force of the organized militia or any reserve force or reserve component of the armed forces of the United States pursuant to orders issued by the competent State or Federal authority.

Requirements

1. Reinstatement Right: All employees of the Douglas County Board of Education, other than those employed on a temporary basis, shall be entitled to military leave for ordered military duty. At the end of such ordered military duty, such employees shall have the right to reinstatement to the position, or substantially equivalent position held, at the beginning of such ordered military duty.
2. Compensation: An employee shall be paid a salary or other compensation for a period of absence while engaged in the performance of ordered military duty and while going to and returning from such duty, not exceeding a total of eighteen (18) days in one federal fiscal year and not exceeding eighteen (18) days in any one continuous period of such absence.

3. State Emergency: In the event the governor declares an emergency and orders an employee to State active duty as a member of the National Guard, such employee shall be paid a salary or other compensation while performing such duty for a period not exceeding thirty (30) days in any one federal fiscal year and not exceeding thirty (30) days in any one continuous period of such State active duty service.
4. National Emergency: In the event the President declares an emergency and orders an employee to active duty as a member of the United States Armed Forces, such employee shall be paid a salary or other compensation while performing such duty for a period not exceeding thirty (30) days in any one federal fiscal year and not exceeding thirty (30) days in any one continuous period of such National active duty service.

FAMILY AND MEDICAL LEAVE ACT

To the extent that any provision in this policy conflicts with or is superseded by the Family and Medical Leave Act ("FMLA"), the regulations promulgated there under, or any other federal law, the provision of the FMLA, its regulations or other law, as the case may be, control.

Administrative Assignments and Duties – Published

Kwame A. Carr, Principal – TMS

Duties and Responsibilities:	Grants	**Supervision of Personnel:**
Safety/Building Security With SRO	Informal & Formal Observations	Math Teachers
LSC/PTA	Instructional Design Plan Implementation	Counselors
Cost Center, Local, Grant, Title 1 Budgets	Teacher Handbook with Adm. Staff	All Clerks
Professional Learning and Staff Development	Testing Coordinator with AP	Adm. Staff
All Personnel	Media Contact	Head Custodian & Night Supervisor
All Personnel Evaluations	Community Affairs	Cafeteria Manager
Curriculum Design/Delivery of Instruction	GPS Implementation	Bookkeeper
Rites of Passage Ceremony with Sponsor	End of Year Procedures(with Adm. Team)	Athletic Director
Public Relations	Hardships	School Psychologist
Strategic Planning	Vertical Teaming	School Social Worker
Heads of Clubs & Organizations	Class Keys Training Coordination	Spec. Ed. Evaluator
Coordinate School Reports	Student Orientation Program	SRO
Instructional (Lead) Support to Teachers	State Compliance	Picture/Yearbook/Uniform Sponsors

All Leaves with A. P.'s Athletic Activities Custodial & Support Staff Cafeteria Staff Bell Schedule(s)	System Compliance All Leave Requests Maintenance & Repair Requests Classroom Video Usage 1st contact	All School Sponsors Buses Master Calendar
Sarah, Assistant Principal **Curriculum & Instruction - D & R**	**John, Assistant Principal** **School Management, Technology & Instruction – D & R**	**Mark,** **Athletic Director**
Curriculum Design & Instruction Instructional Design Plan Implementation Master Schedule (PRIORITY # 1) All Student Schedules (PRIORITY # 1) New Teacher Orientation New Teacher Mentor Program Advanced Placement & TAG Coordination Informal & Formal Observations Professional Learning with Adm. Team Testing Support to Testing Coordinator Teacher Handbook with Adm. Team EOTY Program – Employees of the year GPS Implementation Grading Timelines & Schedules Grading Procedures Schedule Change Coordination SST Coordinator Academic Competitions with Principal Course Syllabi Compliance	Class Coverage in Teacher Absence Parent Portal with front office/M. Spec. Substitute Teacher Assignments Teacher - Substitute Protocols/Binders Student Info. Coordinator. (assist) Safety Coordinator/Drills Book Distribution/Collection/Orders Master Schedule (assist) Testing Coordination Lead New Student Orientation Coordinator of Student Discipline Attendance Protocols & Compliance (for students and teachers) Faculty Handbook Student Handbook Teacher Sign-Ins with Principal Informal & formal observations GPS Implementation/Instruct. Design	Keys Inventories Lockers Student Travel Patterns After School Activities Coord.

Team Teaching Coordination New Student Orientation Program Faculty Handbook (Support) Front office Management with Principal SIS Training/THINKGATE Student Information Coordinator (FTE) Class Coverage (assist) Budgets (assist with Principal) Emergency Leaves DURING School **7th Grade Administrator**	Emergency Leave DURING School Bus Transportation/Stu. Travel Patterns Field Trips Inventories/Facilities Use Agreements Crisis Intervention Team Classroom Video Usage 2nd contact All Duty Schedules/Implementation **6th Grade Administrator** **8th Grade Administrator** Instructional Design Plan Implement.	
Sarah, Assistant Principal **Supervision of Personnel:** Language Arts Teachers Media Assistants Media Specialist Front Office Staff Data Clerk Attendance Clerk TAG/Gifted/Challenge (PC) Special Education Teachers	**John, Assistant Principal** **Supervision of Personnel** Supervise A.D. Supervise SRO Science Teachers Social Studies Teachers Connections Teachers Technology Specialist ISS personnel and protocols	**Mark, Athletic Director** **Supervision of Personnel** All Coaches/Athletic Sponsors

| **Emergency Coverage Plan for Absent Teachers** |

From: Kwame Carr
Sent: Wednesday, July 27, 2011 10:39 AM
To: Turner Middle
Subject: Emergency Coverage Plan for Absent Teachers (Aug. - May)

Greetings,

We know emergencies arise and sometimes substitutes are not readily available. To alleviate random teacher coverage and the over-reliance on the same teachers, this coverage plan is designed to notify all teachers, in advance, of the potential need for coverage during each week throughout the school year. If your name appears during the given week, then please be mentally prepared to cover in cases of emergency. If your name does not appear, then more than likely we will not need your services, **unless** the back-up teacher is also absent.

- Each teacher is assigned one week at a time and four weeks total
- 10 weeks will pass before your services may be needed again
- If your week is a good week, then your services will not be needed, in most cases

Please see the attached rotation for the entire year (use both tabs at the bottom of the spread sheet), **August 4th, 2011 thru May 25th, 2012** and see me personally for all questions regarding this process. It will be further explained during preplanning...

SAMPLE COVERAGE CHART

	1st	2nd	3rd	4th
Aug 4-5	smalls	smalls	kennedy	hall
Aug 8-12	putman	putman	brazil	anderson
Aug 15-19	bulach	bulach	tumilty	tabue
Aug 22-26	digsby	digsby	treubig	kiker
Aug 29 - Sep 2	morgan	morgan	davis	willis
Sep 6-9	london	london	duplessis	woody
Sep 12-16	marshall	marshall	norred	mccann
Sep 19-23	richards	nickle	spiro	camp
Sep 26-29	houston	hutchison	olorunfemi	merchant
Oct 3-7	jones	olorunfemi	padgett	branson
Oct 11-14	smalls	smalls	kennedy	hall
Oct 17-21	putman	putman	brazil	anderson
Oct 24-28	bulach	bulach	tumilty	tabue
Oct 31-Nov 4	digsby	digsby	treubig	kiker
Nov 7-11	morgan	morgan	davis	willis

Weekly Lesson Plan Template

Learning Goals for this Lesson	Standards
Students Will know	**Students will be able to**
Lesson Essential Question	

Activating Strategy
Key Vocabulary to preview and vocabulary strategy

LESSON INSTRUCTION

Learning Activity 1	Graphic Organizer
Assessment Prompt for LA1	
Learning Activity 2	
Assessment Prompt for LA2	Assignment
Learning Activity 3	
Assessment Prompt for LA3	
Summarizing Strategy:	

New Letterhead for New Leadership

TURNER MIDDLE SCHOOL
"The Best Middle School in Georgia"
7101 Turner Drive • Lithia Springs, Georgia 30122

Office: (770) 651-5500   Fax: (770) 651-5503

Mr. Kwame A. Carr, Principal

How to Work in Any Environment – Sample Email Excerpt

From: Kwame Carr
Sent: Wednesday, February 29, 2012 3:59 PM
To: Turner Middle
Subject: FW: How to Work in Any Environment

This is not an attempt to proselytize. Simply put, there's a lot of wisdom contained in these words...

HOW TO WORK IN ANY ENVIRONMENT
(adapted from T.D. Jakes)

1. <u>Maintain professionalism through professional relationships</u>. Don't come to work expecting personal relationships. Expect to be paid for your great service, but don't "expect" much else.
2. <u>Do your job well</u>, but remember your mission. You are here to be a Light.
3. Seek opportunities to change the atmosphere without commenting on the problems. Quietness and <u>competence shall be your strength</u>.
4. Stop going to work to be fed. You didn't come to receive, <u>you came to give</u>.
5. <u>Increase your capacity to work with different personalities</u>.
You will often be blessed through people you don't expect!
6. Remember, <u>where you are does not define where you are going</u>. This will deliver you from frustration. Keep your eye on the prize.
7. Get the optimum results with minimal confusion.
<u>Be effective without making the environment worse</u>.
8. Don't be associated with one group or clique. Labels limit your usefulness.
<u>Work with everybody but be labeled by nobody</u>. Use all your gifts.

Research on Retention

From: Kwame Carr
Subject: Research on Retention of Students - Administrative Position @ TMS

Summary: Overwhelmingly, retention does not work and does not change student behavior. It only makes teachers feel good <u>emotionally</u>, at best.

Despite students' underperformance in a particular grade level, retention of students in that grade level has not proven to motivate students. As a matter of fact, most of these students become discipline problems, give up completely, and perform even worse. The irony in middle school is that we're supposed to build self-esteem among students, even failing ones. As a beginning teacher, I was QUICK to say "retain them." It wasn't long before I learned, personally, and thru research, that retention does not work. Lastly, based on research, teachers usually vote to retain the "bad kids" and **not** the ones with deficits but are NICE. The retention decision tends to be emotionally-driven based on the teacher(s).

Administrative position on retention at Turner Middle School: If a committee of teachers strongly believes a student must be retained, then please know the following:

1. <u>that same student will be on those teachers' schedules the following year for the duration of that year.</u> You know the student best, what works with that student and what does not work.
2. we will not support retaining students and then passing your "problems" on to other teachers on your grade level. Other teachers already have their own "problems."
3. research has already shown that students that are retained are far more likely to drop out of school, especially if there are behavioral issues associated with that student.
4. any student passing the Milestones in a content area they're recommended for retention in will be automatically promoted because that issue speaks to something else.
5. be sure the teacher(s) and the parent(s) are confident retention will change the child for the better and not the worse.
6. retaining 30 out of 200 students, i.e. > 10%, is not realistic educationally, professionally, politically and certainly not economically and will not be supported
7. this is the position administrators will share with parents.
8. administrators reserve the right to override any teacher decision regarding retention, pro or con.
9. we understand many teachers will not agree, and we respect your right to disagree.

Please do the research yourself to see the correlation between retention and future success! I can whole-heartedly embrace our philosophy due to my own research and success as a math teacher at a "tougher" Title 1 middle school which was 99.5% minority with 90% F&R lunch. I had very few failures in math and a high success rate on standardized tests despite teaching students that usually performed multiple grade levels below grade level when they arrived to me in 8th grade. **<u>Retain Wisely!!!</u>**

Top 9 Assignments for Teachers at End of Year

1. Maintain your classroom - discipline - don't burn out - be proactive
2. Remain in charge of your setting and your job description
3. Report to work on time, daily
4. Limit all absences to the minimum, preferably zero - subs can't maintain like YOU
5. Perform all duties as expected - hall duty, door duty, lunch duty, participation in grade level events duty, etc.
6. Finish grades weekly
7. Complete your TMS procedures
8. Enroll in Learning Focus Schools training if you've not taken the required 4 day course
9. Enjoy the break and get some rest and check your email from time to time

Your Day Ends AFTER the Students' Day Ends

From: Kwame Carr
Sent: Tuesday, August 21, 2012 4:08 PM
To: Turner Middle
Subject: Your Day Ends When Students Are Gone

Greetings,

Another moment of clarity...

I've forwarded working hours to the faculty at least two times. The times are sent each year by the superintendent, and I forward them to you. At the bottom of the stated times, **i.e. the small print**, it clearly states that teachers are expected to monitor students thru the end of the day (passed your "clock time," if necessary) to ensure the order and safety of our school. **Students are NOT to be sent to the cafeteria at 4 PM** if they are waiting to ride the bus, yet their bus hasn't arrived. They are to remain with you, the teacher, unless you've made provisions with another teacher to monitor the students on your roster. <u>Any change in this protocol will come directly from me.</u>

Knowing SWD Data (Special Ed.)

109 total students served in the program for exceptional children (up from around 92 last year)

13.7% of total school population

43 - 6th graders are served

34 - 7th graders are served

32 - 8th graders are served

68% of the students with disabilities are served in a general education environment over 80% of the time

14% of students with disabilities are served in a resource class for ELA, Math, and Reading

49% of the students with disabilities are served with supported instruction in Science

7% of the students with disabilities are served with supported instruction in social studies

7% of the students with disabilities are speech only

Most SWD students do not pass science and social studies on the state assessment

What Do I Do The First Day of School And Beyond

From: Kwame Carr
Sent: Saturday, August 4, 2012 1:10 PM
To: Turner Middle
Subject: What do I do the first day of school and beyond?

Procedures for the First Few Days of School (TMS)

- Arrive to work early and sign in

    - Check your mailbox upon arrival for important documents for your records, distribution, information, etc.
    - Report to your assigned room or duty station at 8:10 sharp
    - Only accept students into homeroom listed on your roster, unless directed by an administrator
    - Send students without a homeroom/schedule to ROOM 8
    - Do not exchange students during any period unless approved by Mrs. Fredenburg – all year
    - Homeroom will last until approximately 9-ish AM (Monday and Tuesday)

- 1st period will be shortened on Monday & Tuesday
- Distribute all necessary materials in homeroom
- Follow the attendance protocol for the student count as outlined by administration – Bagby/Cook/Fredenburg
- Be sure every student in your homeroom knows their bus number – contact Mr. Rowe if not
- Allow all students on your roster into class regardless of the time
- Change classes only after administration indicates it's time to change classes
- Do not collect medications from parents or students, send them to the main office
- Review school wide schedule with students during each class, including homeroom
- Review the lunch schedule with students during each class, including homeroom
- Send all returned forms to the front office, i.e. lunch, updated addresses, …
- Report to lunch on time and depart on time – 30 minutes total daily
- Review, enforce, and practice your expectations with students in each class, including homeroom, for the first few days, even into the next week – nip small issues in the bud
- Review breakfast procedures, restroom procedures, locker procedures with all classes - be sure your team is consistent and is covering restrooms
- The Pledge of Allegiance and Silent Reflection will be conducted at 8:20 AM daily via PA - later than usual, however, on Monday and Tuesday
- Afternoon announcements will begin at 3:30 PM daily via PA
- We will dismiss students as usual - do not leave your room until ALL your assigned students are gone
- **Maintain your own positive, WINNING attitude**
- Repeat these procedures daily, excluding extended homeroom
- **Dress Down Fridays will begin August 17th - Lesson Plans are Due August 13th**
- Reinforce the policy of all students reporting to the cafeteria upon arrival to school everyday

Instructional Design – *Principal William Bradley Model*

Instructional Design Plan (IDP) & Professional Development (PD) @ TMS

PRE-TEACHING (Before the lesson…collaboration is required with artifacts as evidence)

1. <u>Collaboratively</u> identify the Power Standards   (**Eliminate this step – D. Co. utilizes Units**)
2. <u>Collaboratively</u> create curriculum maps with standard pacing and an off/pace modified map
3. <u>Individually/Collaboratively</u> study and know your content, vocabulary and skills presented by the standards and elements by:
    a. <u>Individually and collaboratively</u> reading through the standards and associated elements
    b. Making appropriate connections, thinking about possible combinations
    c. Reading through the appropriate sections in the textbook
    d. Reviewing other textbooks and resources
    e. Reviewing the content descriptors (if available) for the standards and elements taught
    f. Identifying and weaving vocabulary into the lesson, referring to them often in context
    g. Recognizing the importance of acquiring vocabulary as it relates to student learning of standards
4. <u>Collaboratively</u> match the levels of cognition with the standard/element
5. <u>Collaboratively</u> organize to teach in ascending order OR order of cognitive rigor and relevance; discuss and recommend a progressive level of questioning
6. <u>Collaboratively</u> create essential and daily focus questions
7. <u>Collaboratively</u> create summative assessments
8. <u>Collaboratively</u> create formative assessments
9. <u>Collaboratively</u> select appropriate instructional strategies – not too many
10. <u>Collaboratively</u> place plan into the required planning format; provide to classroom guests
11. <u>Collaboratively</u> prepare or select lesson documents/artifacts including rubrics; provide to guests

TEACHING (During the lesson…peer observations, modeling, coaching, videotaping, etc.)

12. Teach Your Students by:
    a. Conspicuously posting standards/elements on board or wall and present to students; connect to prior standard or current EQ (essential question)
    b. Conspicuously posting and stating EQ
    c. Unwrapping the standard
    d. Conspicuously posting and stating the FQ (focus question)
    e. Presenting vocabulary in context during the lesson

f. Opening and teaching the acquisition lesson using cognitively appropriate best practice strategy
g. Teaching using cognitively appropriate questions
h. Scaffolding students and fully developing the lesson and concepts being presented to the level of rigor required by the verb in the standard
i. Making relevant real-world connections
j. Conducting mini-summary checks, every 15 minutes (led by teacher(s) and/or students)
k. Closing the lesson
l. Formatively assessing students at the cognitive level taught and use the data to re-teach
m. Re-teaching and/or reinforcing, if necessary
n. Summatively assessing students to determine mastery
o. If no mastery, then re-teach; If mastery, then move on (mastery must be at 80%)

POST-TEACHING **(After the lesson…collaboration is required with artifacts as evidence)**

13. Collaboratively plan to give feedback after the common summative assessment (within 2 – 3 days)
14. Collaboratively decide best use of data to re-teach using a different strategy at the same cognitive level required (may involve extra and personal time – e.g. Response to Intervention)
15. Communicate summative results within 2 to 3 days of the assessment; move on if the mastery number for your subject meets or exceeds expectations. Weigh the need to master vs. the need to move on based on the curriculum map (This requires your professional judgment)

Instructional Strategies

A

Anticipation Guide
Assigned Questions
Author's Chair

B

Balanced Literacy
Book Talks
Brainstorming

C

Case Studies
Categorizing
Classroom Conversations
Cloze Procedure
Clustering
Compare & Contrast
Computer Assisted Instruction
Concept Attainment
Concept Formation
Concept Maps
Conducting Experiments
Cooperative Learning
Creative Problem Solving

D

Debates
Decision-making Process
Demonstrations
Didactic Questions
Discussion
Drill & Practice

E

Essays
Experience Charts
Explicit Teaching
Expository, Narrative & Persuasive Writing

F

Field Observations
Field Trips
Focused Imaging

G

Games
Graphic Organizers
Guided & Assisted Reading
Guided & Assisted Retellings
Guided Reading & Thinking

H

Heterogeneous Grouping
Homogeneous Grouping

I

Independent Research
Inquiry
Instructional Groups
Interdisciplinary Approach
Interviewing

J

Jigsaw
Journal Writing

K

K-W-L

L

Laboratory Groups
Learning Activity Packages
Learning Centers
Learning Contracts
Learning Logs
Lecture
Listen & Visualize
Literacy Centred Instruction
Literature Based Instruction
Literature Circles

M

Mind Mapping
Mini Lessons
Miscue Analysis
Model Building
Modes of Reading
Multiple Intelligence

N

Narrated Reading
Narratives
Needs-based Grouping
Novel Studies

O

Oratory, Public Speaking and Speech Writing

P

Panels
Peer Partner Learning
Picture Books and Illustrator Studies
Picture Word Inductive Model (PWIM)
Probable Passage
Problem Solving

Q

QARs
Questioning Levels
Questioning Techniques

R

RAFT
Read Aloud
Reading for Meaning
Read & Paraphrase
Read & Respond
Read, Pause & Reflect
Readers' Theater
Reciprocal Reading
Reflective Discussion
Reports
Research Projects
Response Journal
Role Playing
Running Record

S

Scaffolding
Science Fairs
Science Olympics
Self Monitoring Strategies
Simulations
SQ3R
Sociograms in Literature
Story Mapping
Storytelling
Structured Controversy
Structured Overview

T

Talking Circles
Team Teaching/Modeling of Instruction
Think Alouds
Think, Pair, Share
Thinking Strategies
Tutorial Groups

Visual Imaging

W

Webbing
WebQuests
Word Walls
Working with Words
Writing to Inform
Write Aloud
Writer's Workshop
Writing Conferences
Writing Process

How to A.C.T. – Administrators, Counselors, Teachers

How to A.C.T.!

Key: A = administrator   C = counselor   T = Teacher/Team

Please note that any discipline issue has the potential to involve an administrator; however, this is usually the case ONLY if the teacher has a student with chronic behavioral issues or has lost control of their classroom environment.

All referrals require a "phone home" REGARDLESS of who completes it.

Behavior	Who will handle behavior
1. Drugs, Alcohol, Tobacco, Weapons	A
2. Forgery/Cheating	T
3. Inappropriate School Behavior	T
4. Fighting	A
5. Theft	A
6. Being in a unauthorized area	T
7. Public display of affection	T
8. Vandalism	A
9. Sex Offenses, gestures, actions, etc.	A
10. Dress code violation	T
11. Profanity between students	T
12. Profanity towards an adult	T then A
13. Arson	A
14. Insubordination	T
15. Horseplay	T
16. Cutting class	T then A
17. Tardiness	T
18. Leaving class/campus	T then A
19. Breaking and entering	A
20. Cafeteria misbehavior	T
21. Open food or beverage, gum, etc.	T
22. Gambling	T
23. Minor disruptions in general	T
24. Inappropriate bus behavior	A
25. Chronic discipline problems	T then A
26. Repeated level III offenses (minor)	T
27. Nuisance item possession (phones)	T
28. Class disruptions	T
29. Failure to serve or complete ISS	A
30. Gang related activity/material	A
31. Threats/Bullying/Talk of Suicide	C
32. Suspected Child Abuse	A, C, T

Strategies for Standardized Tests

Before Testing
- ✓ Go to bed on time.

The Morning of Testing
- ✓ Start your day as you always do.
- ✓ Eat a good breakfast.
- ✓ Think of what you will do to relax after you get home from school.
- ✓ **Think Positive!**

Multiple Choice Questions
- ✓ If you do not understand the directions, ask for help.
- ✓ Read the question and *all* answer choices before marking anything.

Pace Yourself
- ✓ Don't spend too much time on any one question. Do your best and then move on.
- ✓ Answers the easiest questions first, but be sure to go back to those questions you skipped.

Multiple Choice Questions
- ✓ Do not change your answers unless you are very uncertain about your first answer choice.
- ✓ Try to answer every question. Make the most intelligent guess you can.

The Process of Elimination
- ✓ After you have been through all of the questions once, go back and find questions you have some knowledge about and eliminate choices that you know are incorrect.

The Process of Elimination
- ✓ If you can eliminate two wrong answers, your chance of choosing the right answer is greater.

Answering Questions
- ✓ Don't guess blindly, but if you have time to think about the best answer choice, make it!

Skip, Return, Check
- ✓ If you finish early, check to make sure you have answered all questions.

Key Words/Vocabulary
- ✓ Find **key words** or **phrases** in the question that will help you choose the correct answer.

Are we communicating?
- ✓ Make sure you understand what the question is asking.
- ✓ Be sure you are responding to the question that is being asked.

Reading Passages
- ✓ If the test requires you to read passages and then answer questions about what you read, then read the questions first

Reading Passages
- ✓ When there are several questions about a reading passage or chart, look for clues in other questions that will help you with those items about which you are unsure.

Math Computation
- ✓ When using scratch paper on a math test, double check to make sure that you have copied the problem correctly from the test booklet!

Math Computation
- ✓ Line up place value correctly on your scratch paper (thousands, hundreds, tens, ones) or the answer will be incorrect.

Math Computation
- ✓ If your answer does not match one of the choices, reread the problem, recopy the numbers, and try solving it again.

A Matter of Time
- ✓ If any time remains, spend it on those questions about which you know nothing or almost nothing.
- ✓ As you go back through, do not change all answers.
- ✓ *Remember: Your first guess is usually right.*

It's About Time
- ✓ Don't spend too much time rewriting or obsessing about neatness.
- ✓ Don't worry too much if you run out of time, pace yourself accordingly.

Final Tips
- ✓ Fill in bubbles fully, write neatly, and erase stray marks.
- ✓ Double-check the test number in your test booklet against the answer sheet every few questions to be sure you haven't gotten on the wrong number.

The Death Grip
- ✓ If your arm tires during testing it is probably due to the grip that you have on your pencil.
- ✓ Relax the grip and give those muscles a break.
- ✓ Do not do arm exercises during testing as this disturbs others.
- ✓ Remember it's okay not to know everything — unlike class tests, these tests will have some questions designed to challenge the limits of your knowledge at a grade level *above* your current grade.

For Teachers

Design lesson plans and activities to prepare students for standardized tests. Follow the Instructional Design Plan AND the CC/GPS curriculum.

Curriculum Strategies

1. Instructional Portfolio Review/Accountability Binder
2. Data Talks (School-wide – quarterly/annually)
3. THINKGATE usage
4. Common Assessments/Planning by subject or course teams
5. Lesson Plans (formative/summative data based upon SIP targets/goals)
6. Observations with other team members/observations critique with teachers
7. Academic Council formation (chairs, contacts, content)
8. Writing across curriculum (anchor papers, assigned times)
9. Reading across curriculum (selected readings, ITBS questions)
10. Remediation during the day/creative scheduling/ pullouts/support
11. Extended Days
12. Instructional coaches/model lessons/assist students
13. Data Support Specialist
14. Cognitive alignment/Lesson plans/Bloom's/Level of Cognition according to verbs in the standard/Depth of Knowledge
15. Mini-lessons based upon weaknesses
16. Professional learning communities by teams, weekly
17. Sub binders with specifications regularly updated
18. GAPSS analysis of teachers
19. Standards Based Classrooms
20. Instructional Calendars based upon power standards and units
21. Workshops for the bubble students (winter and spring)
22. Competitions
23. Math/Science/Technology Night
24. Clubs
25. School-wide Mock Testing
26. 50% summative assessments/GOFAR
27. Best Practices
28. Instructional Strategies implementation

Planning Process & Lesson Design – Principal Bradley Model

So what should be on the walls of a Standards-Based classroom at TMS?

- Standards and Elements unpacked
- Essential Questions
- Focus Questions
- Content Specific Vocabulary
- Anchor Papers/Rubrics
- Student work samples
- Other things that will help students master the standards

What is the focus in a Standards-Based Classroom?

Traditional Classroom	**Standards-Based**
Teaching focused	Learning focused
Time-based	Competency-based
Fragmented	Interdisciplinary Units
Textbooks	Real World Problems
Routine	Constantly Challenging

The Planning Process

This is a framework (BACKWARDS DESIGN). The actual teaching and learning in a standards-based classroom, as in all classrooms, is the work of the teacher and the student respectively. However, in the standards-based classroom, the teacher does the work prior to beginning a lesson and the student does the work during the lesson to acquire the intended learning. The teacher does the most work during the planning, lesson development, and post-assessment process.

Discipline Process

Turner Middle School

Discipline Infraction Referral Process

Flagrant Infractions	Routine Infractions
Provoking a fight	Disruptive Behavior
Forgery/Altercation of School Form	Failure to Serve Teacher Detention
Assault, Battery, Fighting	Gambling
Skipping Class, Leaving Campus Without Permission	Unexcused Tardies
Inappropriate Language Toward a Staff Member	Inappropriate Languages/Gestures
Smoking, Possession of Tobacco	False Information
Theft, Attempted Theft, Possession of Stolen Property(excludes cells, I-pods, electronic devices)	Cheating
Vandalism of School Property	Writing on a Desk
Possession of Weapons and or Drugs	Public Display of Affection

*All flagrant infractions must result in an immediate referral to the principal, assistant principal, assistant administrator or school resource officer.

I. **Routine infractions** follow the three step referral process outlined below each time an infraction occurs:

Step	Action Taken by the Teacher
1	Warn the student and **call the parent**
2	If the misbehavior continues, assign teacher detention and **contact the parent** to discuss the problem.

Step	Action Taken by the Teacher
3	If the misbehavior continues, **call the parent** and refer the student to the discipline administrator.

II.

Routine infractions for **Special Education Students** follow this five step referral process outlined below **each** time the infraction occurs:

Step	Action Taken by the Teacher
1	Warn the student, visit the students BIP and **call the parent**.
2	If the misbehavior continues, meet with the student's Case Manager and follow the course of action on the BIP, **call the parent**.
3	If the misbehavior continues the Case Manager calls a Behavior Intervention Meeting with the IEP Committee, **advises the parent** that the next step will be a referral to the discipline office.
4	If the misbehavior continues, **call the parent** and refer the student to the discipline administrator.
5	Student's Case Manager, Teacher and Administrator meet to discuss the student's behavior.

Principle 3 – Philosophies

Action Research Findings

Carr's Action Research @ Paul D. West Middle School 2003 (Fulton County, Ga.)

Means of research:

- Reflective Journals (I, too, am bigger)
- Interviews
- Surveys (student/parent)
- Observations
- Discussions
- Checklists

Research Findings:

- ✓ Enact High Expectations
- ✓ Continuous Learners
- ✓ Persistent and Tenacious
- ✓ Competitive Spirit
- ✓ Careful, Flexible Planning
- ✓ Positive Regard for Students
- ✓ Work is Personal and Focused on Learning
- ✓ Maintain Power
- ✓ Predetermined to Succeed Regardless
- ✓ Expert in Content

Action Research Reflections

5 P's: Power, Passion, Preparation, Perspective, Play

What are my own practices?

The practices that stood out the most included: teaching from bell to bell, being prepared daily, refusing to relinquish my power with high discipline expectations and follow through, having the passion to stick with the goals at hand, allowing students to express their perspectives, being competitive, constant assessment, loving my students, etc.

What was the impact on student achievement?

Students were almost forced to learn because downtime was nonexistent. The moment students saw my face, they were summoned to the classroom to begin the day's lesson. I knew that the education process outside of the school building was not guaranteed. Therefore I took every opportunity to make it happen in the classroom. As it turns out, my students began to compete against the high performing students and scored comparably to those attending high performance schools.

Why the Action Research Project (from teacher's perspective)?

The action research project interested me because the principal at my school saw something that stood out among my students. I wasn't sure about the whole process, nor was I really familiar with the concept of action research. Later, I understood that it involved a lot of self-reflection and self-study. I learned that action research would facilitate my own growth as an educator and allow me to see what works and what doesn't work, for me. Action Research provided me with an avenue to actually compete against myself, in the classroom.

Why did I decide to participate?

I decided to participate because the research provided me an opportunity to study my own best practices in the classroom. It enabled me to improve upon those best practices and modify those practices that were not as effective, instructionally. My principal also reassured us that the lessons learned from our research will benefit many educators in the future, especially those working with similar demographics. The study would also potentially increase student achievement, not only in my classroom, but others as well.

What did I know before the Action Research Project?

Before the Action Research Project I thought what most teachers think of themselves, i.e. "I'm a good teacher, I love my subject, and I can teach it."

What do I know now, as a result of the Action Research Project?

As a result of Action Research I now know WHY I'm effective in the classroom. I learned that I've never stereotyped students based upon educational jargon. In my classroom, regular education students, special education students, ESOL students, disciplinary students, socio-economically disadvantaged/advantaged, etc. were all treated the same and expected to perform. In essence, the labels are put away. I learned that my classroom is my domain and that the lessons prepared were well planned based upon student performance with constant formative assessment throughout each lesson. I learned that I'm embarrassed if my students don't perform and I expect for students to learn if I'm indeed to be called a "teacher." I also learned that math is in me and I have an ability to make it plain and simple. It is my true passion.

How did the Action Research Project contribute to my professional development (use teacher & student events as examples)?

Action Research contributed to my professional development because it provided a clear picture of my own practices. It put me in a position to mentor others and become a leader using these practices as a means to explain my own experiences in the classroom. The Action Research project forced me to grow because I'm standing here, today; conveying characteristics that helped me succeed in one of the most challenging middle schools in our system. In that regard, Action Research inevitably made me a public speaker and a facilitator of workshops. As a matter of fact, I think the Project helped me to become an instructional coach. It allowed me to know what works in our schools and share that with others, mathematically speaking.

What did we learn from each other?

I simply learned, or I should say, it reaffirmed the old saying, "there's more than one way to skin a cat!" Each of us approaches our crafts differently. Yet each of us is effective. Teachers are people, and people are different. I learned that there is no cookie cutter approach to good ole fashioned teaching!

Carr's Vision, Mission, Value Statements, Philosophy

VISION

_____ will be the school of choice for the best and brightest students in our community and the school of choice for all students, in general, who seek an exceptional education. _____ is a student-centered school and an academically focused school united with all stakeholders in its commitment to enhancing the quality of life for all students as they become contributing adults to society in the 21st century.

MISSION

Our mission is to add value and to advance the intellectual and social condition of students in our school, and hence our community, state, nation and world, through quality instruction, extra-curricular programs, and progressive stakeholder involvement.

VALUES

Safe and orderly environment

Quality teachers

Standards-based classrooms

Parental involvement

Business partners

PHILOSOPHY

The most ancient structures in the world were built using principles we don't understand. To this day these structures cannot be replicated. In that regard, we are behind the times. People often ask, "How will students ever use this information?" The answer right now is to meet the educational standards set by our nation. Keep in mind that our nation lags behind in achievement on a global scale. We make great strives to abolish illiteracy, yet take comfort and pride in innumeracy.

The gateway to success in education beyond elementary school is the ability to do mathematics. This becomes evident in 8th grade when algebra placement determines the difference between "remedial students" and "on-grade-level" students that take chemistry in high school. Those without the basic foundations in mathematics are not permitted or qualified to enter today's colleges and universities. They are often lost in the competition of our ever-expanding scientific, technological, and data-driven society. They become the achievement gap! The more math you are able to do, the better your life will be, and profit will follow. The at-risk child was born and has always lived in the minds of adults, not in the minds of children!

Spend 1/3 of your life doing what you expected, 1/3 of your life doing more than you expected, and 1/3 of your life doing the unexpected.

How to be a Principal – Baseline Stuff

Design, Enforce, and Communicate the Mission:

Ex: "To prove that students in a non-selective middle school can achieve with adequate support."

Find teachers by asking two questions:

1. How and why do you teach? (Answer: it's my calling)
2. Have you played competitive sports?

Find ONLY people that care, can create a family atmosphere, stays on kids, strong w/discipline

No gimmicks, no programs, no athletics, no high-tech, no commercialization needed

Students must be taught to learn, organize, and take-notes

Obtain baseline data, especially in mathematics and English

Schedule equal time for all content and double dose students in weak areas (math, English, Sci., S.S.)

Discipline – be firm, fair, no-exceptions, the rule is the rule, don't allow little things, high visibility

Administrators – be highly visible, do work after school (emails, conferences, etc.)

3 minute drills – competition among administrators to clear halls in-between classes

Meet kids @ level of proficiency, not @ their level of frustration, then move them up

Allow students to make-up work to earn perfection

Check lesson plans based on a pre-determined schedule for submission, observe teachers

Inspect what you expect

Hire teachers that can get students to sit down, pay attention, and do something creative

Use intuition, intellect, and common sense; school is not the problem, school is a safe-haven

Results are: increased academics and attendance, decreased drop-outs

The Teacher Factor:

- Nothing is more important than the education of our youth; they will run the world
- Are you a professional? Advanced degrees are required for other professions
- Teacher training is the factor
- Don't stress input (programs, teachers, qualifications, technology, etc.)
- It's OUTPUT (<u>can teachers teach our kids?</u>)
- Output dictates accreditation
- Education must be performance based
- Educators must have a shared vision
- The Achievement Gap can be remedied by alignment of assessments for all stake-holders (students, teachers, universities) across the nation

Critical Notes for Educators Taken from My Professors (...actually taken in class)

Dr. Dutton of Lincoln Memorial University

Teachers cannot teach w/o relationships.

Teachers are the most important leaders. It all happens in the classroom.

Modeling is the best teacher.

You can influence with a relationship; leadership requires relationships

Guiding principles:

- Student achievement and behavior = safety/management first
- Every child needs an opportunity to be successful everyday
- Every child needs access to a caring adult everyday

"Weed the garden party every year." Get rid of legacy groups.

Middle schools have been a failed venture (K-8 → need relationships)

In education, steal shamelessly, don't adopt but ADAPT

Am I a life-long learner? (...the answer needs to be YES)

Tell me the last two articles you read that affected your craft!!! (Can you answer?)

Most change is external – MEANINGFUL change is internal

How many schools stop doing things that don't work? Ask WHY five times?

Too much curriculum and extra duties w/o adding more days/time (capacity)

When doing school improvement, START with TIME!

Use speedboats to pull barges – rocks (15%) won't move

- 15% are speedboats
- ½ the speedboats are crazy
- 8% are go-getters
- 70% are willing but not leaders (these are the barges)

Vocabulary is the foundation of all instruction.

Don't put new teachers next to rocks

No consistent research that justifies technology; Marzano and interactive white boards

Page 72

Most important thing that principals do is hire and fire teachers

Principals must renew teachers around 15 to 20 year mark – involve teachers

Imagine what I'd (you'd) do if I (you) weren't afraid?

Can't be an academic leader AND a butt-kicker; not enough energy/time in a day

One white hat and one black hat as assistant principal/principal

Most poorly distributed resource in public education is good teachers

Who typically gets the new teachers or the sorry teachers?

Assessment drives instruction; it tells teachers what to teach and re-teach

Assessment, historically, has been used to determine grades

Advanced Placement model of assessment is a great example of true assessment

Must have common practices in curriculum, instruction, assessment, and organization

Curriculum is the place to start when students are struggling NOT with instruction

The silver bullet is in capacity building within the school, use what you have!

Guiding principles that drive principals and schools:

- Trust and relationships
- Listening
- Focus and Goals
- Pareto Rule (20/80 rule)
- Empowerment
- Accountability

Critical Notes for Educators:

Dr. Dutton of Lincoln Memorial University

Two ways to make a decision – by philosophy or situation

Turn abstract into concrete for students

Your life is out of balance if you're not thinking about what you're doing

Teachers must plan well in advance and plan together

Leadership begins with vision, manifests through self-discipline, then impacts others

Leadership styles:

- Visionary   +
- Coaching   +
- Affiliative +   Use them all when needed
- Democratic   +
- Pacesetting -
- Coercive   -

The law of the farm → meaningful stuff never occurs quickly (weed and seed)

Meaningful change occurs inside first – outside last

No such thing as extrinsic motivation; it's all intrinsic – there's only extrinsic stimuli

The part of brain that gets angry and the part that thinks are separate

You can't scare people into doing the right thing; anger is involuntary; thinking is voluntary

New principals think everything counts; figure out the right stuff and work on that

Good coaching staffs are the best learners; faculties must adopt sports coaching models

(I.e. constant inquiry and evaluation)

Focus and purpose is key; become thoughtful about what we do; know why we do it

Map curriculum from 1ˢᵗ day of school <u>to the test</u>

Staff development – minimize sit and get; use coaching models

Praise in public; reprimand in private; don't praise new teachers in public too soon

Building self-esteem requires zapping people about small things and large

Celebrations reveal your values

Celebrate academics

Today's kids need someone to listen

Can't empower people; people empower themselves; create conditions for empowerment

Managers	Leaders
Administers	Innovates
Copy	Original
Maintains	Develops
Accepts	Investigates
System Structures	People
Control	Trust
Short Range View	Long Range Perspective
How and When	What and Why
Eye on Bottom Line	Eye on Horizon
Accepts Status Quo	Challenges Status Quo
Good Soldier	Own Person
Does things right	Does right things
Imitates	Originates

Critical Notes for Educators:

Dr. Dutton of Lincoln Memorial University

Managers are necessary; leaders are essential

Management is of mind; leadership is of the spirit

Can't lead an organization that doesn't have goals

The more prescriptive we become about at-risk interventions, the less freedom 4 teachers

Three kinds of decisions:

- Leader decides
- Leadership decides
- Vote

Every principal needs a leadership team; two ways to design a leadership team:

- Selected in
- Voted in

The most empowering tool for students is choice

Teachers calling students "irresponsible" really means students aren't being compliant

Trust is gained verbally; non-trust is facilitated in writing (i.e. to CYA) – to cover your ass

We hand out choices in life with education

Difference between principles and values:

- Principles don't change
- Values change

Critical Notes for Educators:

Dr. J. Murphy (Lecturer and Researcher of Achievement Gaps)

Changes coming from outside pressure; these pressures shape leadership

1890 – 1920 was the last time this type of educational revolution has been recorded

We're in the midst of educational reform in 2011

Contributors to reform movement:

- Economy (economic conditions)
- Social environments
- Political climate
- Technology

These factors shape education and what we do; i.e. in the schooling enterprise

Economic pressures brought about the "standards movement"

We graduate students at an 8th grade level (based upon the world measure):

- 1/3 do really well
- 30% meet the goal
- 25% don't make it
- Higher % of failure in urban schools
- 47% blacks graduate nationwide; 28% in N.Y. etc.
- 1880 – 1990 there was an unbroken faith that gov. would handle problems (social issues)

Began to change during Reagan era (mid 1980's)

1990 there were zero charter schools nationwide!!!

Politics changed and charter schools opened

Market/Consumer approach to education is changing education due to political changes

We work in last business that opens and closes its doors based on employee needs

This approach is not in alignment with the market/consumer driven society

We are in the midst of the 2nd Educational Revolution

1920 – 2000 there were two variable in education: Teaching and Learning

For 100 years the focus was on Teaching

Today <u>Learning</u> is the focus!

Curriculum was differentiated; i.e. tracking of students

Today: Instruction is differentiated while holding curriculum the same, regardless

<u>Structural Changes such as: block scheduling, team-teaching, looping, cooperative learning, PLCs, academies, advisement, etc. WON'T change teaching and learning, and have not thus far</u>

The right DNA must come with the "program"

Behavioral perspective has deep roots in education ("200 miles deep, 60 miles wide")

Behavioral perspective says teachers are expected to pour knowledge into students

Structural change WILL NOT predict performance or increase performance

Seed Bed must change!!! Plant seeds based upon what you want to grow

The fundamental belief in education = learning/teaching based knowledge transmission

Another fundamental belief is that students learn individually

Standardized tests serve the purpose of spreading kids (scores) out

Two types of achievement gaps:

- Blacks and Whites
- Socio-economic

Why is the achievement gap important and what is the impact?

- If you're behind, you're going to stay behind! (you can't pull someone off a moving train and still expect to get there on time)
- Limited career choices and paths
- Concentration in lower-paying jobs
- Reduced economic competitiveness
- Reinforces social inequities

[RULES OF ENGAGEMENT FOR CLOSING ACHIEVEMENT GAP]

<u>Four sets of findings:</u>

1. Big picture conclusions
2. Factors to emphasize
3. Timing
4. Caution

Schools don't close achievement gaps; gaps rooted in poverty, not race; starts at grade K

To begin closing the achievement gap, begin with summer learning

Critical Notes for Educators:

Dr. J. Murphy (Lecturer and Researcher of Achievement Gaps)

Target kids challenged by the gap

Schools cannot close the achievement gap alone

Historically the achievement gap has not been a front-burner issue

There was an unwillingness to see the issue in ethical terms

There was a reluctance to reset priorities and reallocate resources

Low-income and minority students are more school-dependent

Schools can HELP solve the problems

Poverty is a rural problem; 60% to 70% of poverty is rural

Focus on both out of school and in-school factors

A combination of factors is needed to close the achievement gap:

- Better instruction (40%)
- Stronger school culture; an academic press for success
- Lower class sizes at lower grade levels
- More personalization and better relationships
- Greater curricular rigor
- More intensive support

Focus on instructional program AND culture

Strategies for closing the achievement gap that work:

1. pre-school
2. cooperative instructional strategies
3. smaller class sizes
4. **quality instruction ***
5. co-curricular/extra-curricular activities
6. more rigorous courses
7. placement in high SES schools; i.e. mix students among socio-economic status
8. minority teachers with minorities; working class teachers
9. parents help with homework
10. service learning
11. high teacher expectations
12. supportive environments, risk-free environments, safe and orderly environments

13. classroom management/opportunity to learn*
14. an integrated, coherent, cohesive, overlapping instructional model is best
    [50% of 9th graders fail nationwide]

15. after school tutoring program
16. 9th grade academy after summer support
17. acceleration and remediation design
18. master teachers
19. extra services; double dosing sessions (add time)
20. extending schooling
21. pre-loading learning/ VOCABULARY
22. faculty advisors/counseling

KEEP KIDS ON THE TRAIN AND DON'T RETAIN!!!!!

There is no short-term solution!

Early interventions TRUMP latter interventions (age-wise)

Higher teacher expectations for K-4; teacher has bigger effect/has kids' attention at that age

High personalization in 8 – 12

Prevention TRUMPS remediation

Keep kids moving w/their class! (Pre-load using previewing strategies, e.g. advance organizers)

Do not withdraw student support once gains are made or resources are cut

Focus on achievement – level; equity; value-added

Critical Notes for Educators:

Fulton County Schools Promising Principal Program Notes 2011 (3P)

(Budgeting)

State revenue is 35% of budget

Property taxes = 65% of budget

$800 million budget

85% tied to personnel

15% tied to utilities, transportation, etc.

Safety and security is first

Contracting deals with money being spent properly

Site-based budgeting is practiced in Fulton County

Principal monitors budget solely

Review cost-center guidelines often

(Operations)

1,300 employees in this department

Buses, Nutrition, Maintenance, Environmental Services, Utilities

(Introduction)

Principals need instructional leaders on the team; articulation is key; collaborative group

7 key strategies must permeate school/classroom

Malcolm Gladwell wrote Outliers – practice makes perfect; 10,000 hour theory

Article on Overloaded Circuits:

- multi-tasking is a myth
- the more info you collect the poorer the decision
- brain needs time to process things unconsciously to make a better decision
- "less is more"

Beware the busy manager; people that look the busiest get the least done!

Taking one thing at a time works better than multi-tasking

(School Board)

For Board members to be successful, schools must be successful

School Boards are ultimately held accountable

<u>Principals MUST:</u>

- Have partnerships with the community
- Have a good relationship with PTA and LSC
- Treat employees right
- Keep a great budget and a great bookkeeper
- Make relationships with feeder schools
- Call area superintendent when in trouble; especially if lawsuit is possible

(Speaking Engagements)

- Always talk about children/students
- Always reveal the human element
- Always reveal inner passion
- Always get to the point; BE CONCISE
- Avoid filler words and slang words
- Avoid using acronyms that the audience may be unfamiliar with
- Remember people are always listening!
- Always introduce yourself
- Avoid using student names in public
- Avoid the use of "God" in politics
- Use research but KNOW the research
- Use connection with the community
- (Accountability Office)
- You're either green and growing or ripe and rotten
- The principal-ship is really not like what I thought it would be… (The Ultimate Realization!!!)
- Face to face time is crucial for every decision – talk to everybody
- Be aware of the value-added system and what it measures – compares apples to apples

Critical Notes for Educators:

Dr. Dutton of Lincoln Memorial University

Instruction is not always priority

Curriculum is ALWAYS priority

Are we teaching the right stuff? Are we assessing correctly?

Are we assessing to IMPROVE or are we assessing to PROVE?

Project Star studied 6000 students from grade K using class sizes:

- [15:1 student-teacher ratio] and [25:1 student-teacher ratio] and [25:1 w/a student assistant]
- Project Star studied achievement of students in grade K
- Effects of quality instruction washed out by grade 3
- However, quality effects from K resurfaced in H.S. and college and as adults; divorce rates too
- Bad teachers NEVER wash out; two years of bad teachers and you're done (esp. in math)
- Algebra 1 is the foundation class for chemistry
- Lowest achievement mode [25:1 student-teacher ratio w/ teacher assistant]
- **Lowest students are typically sent to the teacher assistant, where they continually fall behind; co-teaching model yields similar results and is deemed ineffective*****************

HOPE Conference Notes 2007 – Marietta, GA (…actually taken during the conference)

Tom Guskey

Using Standards & Assessment to Improve Student Learning

Standards Based Education: (Four Crucial Understandings)

1. The Ideas are NOT new
   Ralph W. Tyler (1949) – Bloom's Teacher wrote "Basic Principles of Curr. & Instr.)

   A. Two decisions
      i. What do I want students to learn?
      ii. What evidence is sufficient that will verify they learned it?
   B. We can no longer say
      i. I taught them they didn't learn it!
      ii. I sold it they just didn't buy it!
      iii. I taught them to swim they just keep sinking!
2. The Ideas are more important than the vocabulary: Testing → Assessment
3. Good ideas CAN be implemented poorly
   A. How do the ideas translate into practice?
   B. How will you know if they work?
4. Success in education hinges on what happens at the CLASSROOM level

Guidelines for SUCCESS:

1. Think BIG, but start small. Don't require too much, too soon from teachers and administrators
2. Ensure that assessment becomes an INTEGRAL part of the instructional process
   a. Quizzes/Tests are learning tools
   b. They are not simply evaluation tools that mark the end of learning
   c. Spiral instruction through review

IMPLICATION #1 → Assessments must be sources of information for students and teachers. Assessments must NOT be secret!!! If half the students missed a problem, then that's not a student problem, it's a TEACHER problem.

IMPLICATION #2 → Assessment must be followed by HIGH QUALITY Corrective Instruction (this is not re-teaching using the same method that didn't work the 1st time!)

IMPLICATION #3 → Students MUST be given a second chance to show improvement

(Examples: Doctors, Lawyers, Pilots, etc.)

Quote: Spectacular achievements are always preceded by unspectacular preparation

Roger Staubach – quarterback

Where will the time come from???

      i. The first units WILL take more time
      ii. Corrective work MUST be overseen in the beginning
      iii. Students will catch on and eventually corrective work will be accomplished independently at home (This is a slow process but it saves time in the long run)

What's the motivation to get it right the 1st TIME if they know they have a 2nd chance???

      i. Certificates (sizes, colors, stars, etc. that represent success)
      ii. "Tangible evidence of success"

Group Based instruction facilitated by the teacher is necessary. Always spiral instruction for those that don't get it and to keep difficult concepts fresh. If students don't get it after the second chance then MOVE ON!!!

      i. Recall Kindergarten Example (Run and Touch the Wall)

Managers know how to do things right!

Leaders know the right things to do!

Alan Blanstein

Failure Is Not an Option

"I'll do anything to get my students in the class." (Recall the dancing example)

Four Assumptions:

1. Everyone is already working hard
2. Every school has some excellent teachers
3. It's an internal journey – most of what you need is already there
4. The real challenge is finding the unifying purpose

3 Components of Failure is Not an Option:

Why? Failure is Not an option for any student

What? Sustainable Learning Communities

Who? Courageous Leaders

1. Teachers pursue a clear, shared purpose for all students' learning
2. Teachers engage in collaborative activity to achieve their stated purpose
3. Teachers take collective responsibility for all students' learning

FOUR TYPES OF COLLABORATIVE TEAMS

1. Individualistic
2. Balkanization
3. Contrived Collegiality
4. Collaboration

REVIEW 20 WAYS OF CONNECTING WITH STUDENTS:

1. Greet students at the door
2. Commenting positively on non-academics
3. Catching "carry-in" problems
4. Writing home to congratulate parents
5. Calling on students randomly
6. etc. (see handout)

Homework must be reinforcement of what's already learned!!!

Stephen Peters

Five Major Influences:

50's	80's	90's	Present
Home	Home	Peers	Media/TV
School	Peers	TV	Peers
Church	TV	Home	School
Peers	School	School	Church
TV	Church	Church	Home

Today's students require their permission to teach them!!!!

Who taught you? How do you know you're ready? – Because YOU taught me!

The teacher told me I was smart, "So I Was!"

Nobody RISES to low expectations.

Creating a culture of success requires: phenomenal teachers, support staff, custodians, cafeteria staff, etc.

Three Step Process:

1. Capture (Who is your favorite teacher? – Why?)
2. Inspire (Dress, gain allies, etc.)
3. Teach

Dr. Deborah Wortham

Use energizers!

Change your behavior or get off the bus. Bring adults together for the good of student achievement (holding hands example – Love Circle)

The achievement gap is NOT between the students, it's between the professionals

Put the answers on their bodies → use songs and hand signals and games

Mission = what's in the heart

Vision = what's the end product

Values = what are we willing to fight for

Goals = what are the steps we need to take

Market your Mission!!!

Eliminate Faculty Meetings; Have them during the Day

Provide snacks, sodas, water, refreshments, to teachers

Provide a Feedback Form for teachers to address → "What I understand"

→ "What I'm wondering"

Spend 50% of your day in the classrooms – put on your "ugly shoes" – you can't be a phantom administrator

Keep a tally of teachers observed weekly to ensure all teachers are seen multiple times

Tell teachers the TRUTH!

As office referrals go down, student achievement GOES UP!!!

Graduation Coach Notes from Ga. Conference 2011:

The workplace skill set is very similar to the college skill set (mathematics and communication)

32% of High School graduates have mastered BASIC literacy skills and coursework necessary to succeed in a 4 year college (ACT, 2004)

High levels classes work best; low level courses don't work → They quality of courses completed in H.S. is a greater predictor of college success than test scores, class rank, or grade point average

"The is an inverse relationship between academic success and discipline"

Students are more likely to pass high level courses than low level courses, even when low level students are taking high level courses

Use TAA models – Teachers as Advisors

Use connections for support and ELIMINATE tracking

2008 → Math = 66.7% passing state assessment

2008 → Language Arts/Reading = 73.3% passing state assessment

If not me, then who?

If not now, then when?

81% of inmates have no high school diploma

94% of students who drop out will be rejected for a job

2000 students dropped out of school in 2006-2007 BEFORE 8th grade

3rd grade reading determines prison bed allocations

Coaching duties and responsibilities:

1. Advisement – using best practices
2. Transitions – between elementary, middle, and high school
3. Awareness – catching at-risk students early
4. Parent Connections – keeping parents involved

Graduation Teams:

→ Help identify at-risk students, assess school and student needs, and develop/coordinate appropriate interventions

Coaches work with faculty/administration to develop a grade recovery program

Strategies:

Individual tutoring sessions, lock-ins (weekends), after hours tutorial, individual attention, wake-up calls, breakfast on test day, etc…

Principle 4 – House Rules

Leadership Decisions

From: Kwame Carr
Sent: Friday, August 23, 2013 9:50 AM
To: Turner Middle
Subject: Leadership Decisions

Certain personnel have been assigned by administration and are entrusted to lead various aspects of TMS with minimal interference from administration. As long as they are doing their job, leading effectively and **getting results**, I stay out of it.

Here's an abbreviated list of things I purposely stay out of, in alphabetical order:

- Assessment Leadership (Testing)
- Athletic Leadership (Sports)
- Cafeteria Leadership
- Content Area Leadership
- Custodial Leadership
- Departmental Leadership
- Grade Level Leadership
- Media Center/Technology Leadership

Unless there is a dire emergency, an ethics complaint or hard data proving lack of effectiveness, please resolve issues/conflicts within the realm of leadership in question.

Clarifying Announcements

From: Kwame Carr
Sent: Monday, August 8, 2011 1:29 PM
Subject: Afternoon Announcement Change (Buses/Car-riders/Walkers)

Greetings,

I realize in the past Mr. Collins did afternoon bus announcements; however, most of my announcements will occur in the morning time during homeroom via PA. I prefer to set the tone whenever I'm available early each morning. With that said, I am releasing bus announcements to Mr. Rowe, who has suggested alternative announcers, in this order of availability:

1. Mr. Kruzinski
2. Mr. J. Lewis
3. Mr. Merchant
4. Mr. Rowe
5. Mr. Carr

Changing Bus Routine /Afterschool Dismissal/Regaining Control

From: Kwame Carr
Sent: Tuesday, August 16, 2011 5:14 AM
To: Turner Middle
Subject: I'm changing buses and PE today (ACTION REQUIRED)

Greetings Turner,

Like I stated during pre-planning, I am going to watch and perhaps change some things as we go along. Here are immediate changes beginning Tuesday, Aug. 16, 2011.

Bus Dismissal - for every teacher to implement - everyone has bus duty

Due to the increasing number of students missing buses, students standing outside waiting for buses, and students leaving on the wrong load, we are implementing the following:

- **Only students whose bus is called will be released**, all other students must remain in the classroom, until the very last bus is called (core content classes and connections)
- When a bus number is called, students must exit expeditiously to board the bus before it departs
- Students will NOT report to the cafeteria en mass unless they are an after school car rider or in after school tutoring, which hasn't started- no exceptions
- All teachers and students need to **listen** to all announced buses, as well as teachers on duty, who will be strategically placed throughout the building
- Students departing at the wrong time will be directed back to their teacher's class immediately by administrators and teachers on duty
- Yes, this means teachers with a 7th period will house their class for orderliness and safety reasons, school-wide - **do not send any bus riders to the cafeteria**
- There is no first load, first phase, second load, second phase release anymore - that is confusing - there is only one strategic "bus dismissal," by bus(es)
- I will announce buses and procedures the remainder of this week and Mr. Kruzinski will resume next week
- Bus dismissal will begin at 3:26 PM each day
- The first four buses will be called as usual, i.e. the "four return buses," along with walkers and car riders
- ALL remaining buses will be called as they arrive - **Hold all students until their specific bus is called** - teachers are released when their last student leaves

7th Period PE - for Merchant, McCann, Branson, and Camp

Due to back to back to back incidences in PE with 8th graders during 7th period only, we will do the following in 7th period only:

- These students will not dress out for PE the remainder of this week, they will meet with me in the cafeteria at 3PM sharp
- PE teachers must take roll in the gym and quietly and orderly walk PE students to the cafeteria by 3PM Wednesday, Thursday and Friday of this week
- Tuesday (today) is picture day and students will not dress out anyway - if that was the plan, then please don't dress out - follow the picture day plan
- PE teachers, please meet with me during 4th period planning, during 8th grade lunch in the cafeteria, Tuesday, Aug. 16, 2011 (today)

Publishing Bus Numbers

From: Kwame Carr
Sent: Tuesday, August 16, 2011 4:34 PM
To: Turner Middle
Subject: Daily Bus Numbers

1. **245 returns for another load**
2. **259 returns for another load**
3. **307 returns for another load**
4. **221 returns for another load**
5. **348**
6. **295**
7. **195**
8. **298**
9. **342**
10. **372**
11. **243**
12. **245**
13. **259**
14. **307**
15. **221**

These buses are not necessarily announced in the order presented above, so please listen daily and WRITE the buses as they're called on the board daily. Thanks!

School Program Protocol

From: Kwame Carr
To: Turner Middle

Greetings,

From time to time we will have school-wide assemblies, pep rallies, presentations, celebrations, etc. Here is our standard protocol for such events:

1. prior approval from the principal, at least a month in advance, barring unforeseen celebrations such as a play-off game pep rally, ...
2. teachers must have at least two weeks notification to adequately plan instruction and reflect such on their lesson plans

Miscellaneous Discipline Protocols

From: Kwame Carr
Sent: Tuesday, October 4, 2011 1:42 PM
To: Turner Middle
Subject: What do teachers do when... (action required)

Greetings Teachers,

After reviewing, questioning, and reflecting on policies, the following protocols are to be implemented at Turner, effective Wednesday, October 5, 2011:

"My students have piercings in uncommon places" (i.e. other than the ears)

Teachers must first inform the parent/guardian by calling or simply verifying that parents know; teachers know who have new piercings, administrators don't. Furthermore, parents are to be reminded that such piercings are prohibited by Douglas County Schools. Students continuing to wear such piercings will receive consequences for insubordination. Please submit your referral to the proper administrator as such, but FIRST reiterate to students that our newly enforced policy is totally aligned to Douglas County Schools. Additionally, continuing to wear such items will result in continued and immediate suspension.

"My students have unnaturally colored hair or creative hairstyles"

Do Nothing - other schools don't really bother with hairstyles and neither will we

"My students drink energy drinks"

Do Nothing - it's not against the law. I've already conferred with County Office in this matter, and they support these protocols at Turner Middle School...

Technology Protocols

From: Kwame Carr
Sent: Thursday, December 8, 2011 9:30 AM
To: Turner Middle
Subject: New Technology Protocol

As we order and receive new technology at Turner, large and small, it is expected that students AND faculty AND staff will take proper care of the equipment. That means students must be regularly told and reminded how to handle these items (head phones, CDs, keyboards, Active Boards, Slates, Acti-Votes, computer monitors, passwords, etc.).

Any adult that is in charge of students and is responsible for monitoring students is also in charge, responsible and accountable for our technology equipment if they choose to allow students under their care to use this equipment.

Cafeteria Rules – 30 minutes

From: Kwame Carr
Sent: Tuesday, August 14, 2012 12:26 PM
To: Turner Middle
Subject: One New Rule...for lunch

Greetings,

As you know, lunch is 30 minutes or a little more. Sometimes there are delays in serving lunch due to a cafeteria worker shortage or the types of items being served or some combination thereof. Extending lunch beyond the allocated time impacts the next lunch and the lunch after that, if applicable. Extending lunch impacts available seats, congestion in the cafe' and entrance/exit strategies. Extending lunch also impacts fifth period class time and class transitions and requires an immediate emergency response, as the length of the delay can't be determined. Extending lunch also impacts cafeteria employees' working hours.

The solution is SIMPLE:

1. We <u>will not</u> extend lunch beyond the posted times, please exit on time daily (Rule # 1)
2. If a class or if classes face minimal "eat time," then take the class and your lunch back to your classroom and vacate the cafeteria on time (New Rule # 2)

This will not happen often, but when it does, please vacate on time.

Parents Demanding an Immediate Meeting

How to Meet UNANNOUNCED with Teachers/Administrators at TMS

It is our pleasure to serve you and your child(ren) at Turner Middle School. We have an average sized middle school, which means we deal with many situations and families every single day. Most of our minutes during each day entail preplanned meetings, protocols and operations to ensure a safe, supportive environment conducive for learning. Parental involvement is important to us; however, please understand that unannounced visits cannot always be immediately accommodated due to prior appointments and obligations. We will do our best to meet all concerns in a timely fashion, but the order of unannounced meetings must be prioritized by appointment, necessity and/or on an emergency basis. The protocol to meet with our personnel is as follows:

To Meet with Teachers

Your first contact to resolve issues with a teacher is the teacher. Teachers require a 24 hour notice before anyone is allowed into their classroom, unless previous arrangements have been made with that teacher. Emails and voicemails are fine and are expected to be answered within 36 hours by the teacher. Please do not expect a teacher to meet on the spot without notice unless it is an emergency. The administration will determine emergencies. In many cases teachers will meet with parents on the spot; however, please understand that once they arrive to school, teachers have duties and responsibilities to perform each morning. Parents have the right to meet with teachers one on one in a location designated by the teacher. Teachers may opt to meet:

- before school
- during planning time, but not during instructional time, unless approved by administration
- after school

To Meet with Assistant Principals

Assistant principals have duties that are required to ensure efficiency in our school operations, and they also oversee all teachers and students. In general, assistant principals are not available:

- 8:00 AM through 8:30 AM when students are arriving
- during hallway transitions between classes
- after school between 3:20 PM until 3:50 PM

Appointments are encouraged, as assistant principals also have prearranged obligations. Assistant principals will do their best to resolve all issues arising with students, teachers and/or parents in a timely manner, depending upon urgency.

To Meet with the Principal

The principal has the same schedule as assistant principals and meets with parents by appointment. Issues with teachers must first be addressed with that teacher. If a resolution is not agreed upon, the parent may appeal to an assistant principal. If a resolution with the assistant principal is not agreed upon, then a meeting with the principal may be gained through appointment on a prioritized basis. In cases of true emergency, the principal will meet with parents unannounced.

"Go Get a Pass" is not allowed

From: Kwame Carr
Sent: Wednesday, August 29, 2012 2:35 PM
To: Turner Middle
Subject: "Go Get a Pass" - Lockers - Restroom - Tardiness - Let Them In

Greetings,

These are our protocols:

1. **"Go Get a Pass"** - We don't send students back out in the hall to a teacher's class to retrieve a pass. This wastes even more instructional time and clutters the hall and disturbs both teachers. Late students are to be admitted. If they are becoming a "tardy issue," call the parent, assign detention and take other proactive steps to rectify the situation, with the last resort being a referral to the grade level administrator. Keep your power!
2. **Lockers** - Encourage students to use lockers wisely and in a timely fashion by accessing them during strategic times of the day. We have many more students using lockers this year.
3. **Restroom** - This has already been addressed in detail
4. **Tardiness** - It is not appropriate to send a student anywhere when they're tardy by a second or 30 seconds. I will be visible all year to keep students moving during transitions. This responsibility belongs to ALL of us. Many of you do a great job moving students. The goal is to master the three minute transition; however, the REAL goal is to maximize student time on task and classroom instructional time.
5. **Intentional Tardiness** - Release students when the bell rings to ensure a consistent, organized flow to our school. Plan your lessons accordingly and don't cause student tardiness.
6. **Let Them In** - Students need to be in class when the bell sounds or very nearby moving quickly to get there. Lining students up in the hall prior to the bell is not our protocol. Bringing students back out into the hall after they go in the classroom is not our protocol, unless you're going to another destination, like a lab or the media center. Management of assigned students is our protocol. This is the fourth week of school and the tone for each classroom needs to have been set by now.

Framing Pep Rallies

From: Kwame Carr
Sent: Tuesday, September 4, 2012 12:45 PM
To: Turner Middle
Subject: Friday's Schedule 9-7-2012 (Pep Rally during 7th Period)

Greetings,

Although faculty will design the program for Friday's pep rally, I've taken the liberty to create the schedule. **We will report back to 7th period immediately after the pep rally for regular dismissal,** just as we did last year, i.e. back to class. Please plan accordingly and share this expectation and procedure with students prior to Friday. We no longer have the ability to stop and start the bells manually. <u>They ring regardless,</u> so it's best we stick by the regular day schedule and chalk up 7th to avoid confusion. Thank you...

Pep Rally – Sept. 7, 2012

- 08:09 bell rings to dismiss students from cafeteria to homeroom –
- 08:27 homeroom ends
- 08:30 1st period begins
- 09:20 1st period ends
- 09:23 2nd period begins
- 10:13 2nd period ends
- 10:16 3rd period begins
- 11:06 3rd period ends
- 11:09 4th period begins/6th reports to A-lunch as soon as possible and leaves by 11:42
- 11:43 4th period continues/7th reports to B-lunch and leaves by 12:15
- 12:17 4th period continues/8th reports to C-lunch and leaves C-lunch by 12:47
- 12:50 4th period ends
- 12:53 5th period begins
- 01:43 5th period ends
- 01:46 6th period begins
    - 02:20 {BAND MEMBERS AND OTHER PERFORMERS REPORT TO WILLIS}
- 02:36 6th period ends – {ATHLETES REPORT TO MERCHANT}
- 02:39 7th period begins – 7th period is very short - take attendance
    - 02:41 {All students dismissed via PA to the gym to be seated}
    - 02:51 {Pep Rally <u>Promptly</u> Begins...}
    - 03:16 {Pep Rally <u>Promptly</u> Ends...} Students Orderly Report back to 7th
- 03:30 Normal dismissal from 7th period class via PA

Hiring New Teachers and Assigning Responsibility

From: Kwame Carr
Sent: Monday, November 3, 2014 1:46 PM
Subject: New Hire Protocol @ TMS : Updated

This year in particular, we've had to acclimate new personnel to our campus. So that our expectations are clear from the beginning, I am herewith making the following assignments. New teachers must be provided resources and training by the following personnel **within the first 5 business days of their initial contract.**

- Grading Policy / Grade Book Set-Up / SST — Fredenburg
- Absence Protocol — Cook
- Substitute Protocols (binders) — Rowe
- Safety Protocols — Rowe
- Lesson Plan Format/Expectations — Lobban
- Student Passes/Discipline/Restrooms — Assigned Grade Level AP
- Instructional Models — Lobban
- Team Issues/Expectations — Grade Level/Department Chair
- RTI — Grade Level Counselor

Grades and SWD (Special Ed.)

From: Sean (**Special Education Chairperson**)
Sent: Thursday, November 13, 2014 1:19 PM
To: Turner Middle
Subject: SWD and Grades

1. When assigning grades to special education students please be sure that you are following through on all students supports. For example but not limited to:

   - If their IEP calls for retaking a test allow them to retake after remediation
   - Make sure if you are to supply teacher notes that you are doing so
   - If they need read aloud, extended time, small group support for tests make sure they are getting it (If you need para help for this please let me know).
   - Cue to task
   - Notify Parent and case manager

2. Students should not receive a passing grade for doing nothing in your class, if you have followed all student supports in IEP it is permissible to fail a student with a disability. If you see a student in danger of failing, I would appreciate it if you let me know as well.

3. Co-teachers communicate grades to each other in order to ensure that you are on the same page when it comes to grades for students with disabilities.

Preparing Sub Folder(s) in a Red Binder

Welcome letter
Lesson plans for the day or period of absence
Class rosters
Classroom procedures
Layout of the room seating charts
Classroom rules
Schedule for the day include lunches, connections
Emergency drill/situation procedures
Map of school
List of students to help with procedures
Place to send students not the office
Alternative plans i.e., rain routes,
Paper for notes and reports of day's events.

Failing Grades Require Parent Contact

From: Kwame Carr
Sent: Wednesday, August 28, 2013 12:24 PM
To: Turner Middle
Subject: Teachers : Failing Grade(s) & Parent Contact Forms Due on Sept. 6, 2013 to Carr by 3:30 PM

As a reminder, students failing at each 4 1/2 week grade report must have a parent contact logged into your **records by each teacher**. Attached is one example of a parent contact form. You may use your own; however, your parent contact must be made on the basis of the current grade at 4 1/2 weeks (i.e. not discipline, not your introductory call, not regarding a workshop, etc.). There must be a one-to-one correspondence between students failing and students with parent contact concerning the failure. Parental contact is acceptable using the following correspondence mediums, in this **order of preference**:

1. **Phone call** - with date/time documented - person spoken to documented
2. Email documented
3. Personal Letter with return signature documented
4. Agenda message is the LEAST preferred, especially if the agenda has not been effective for the student for other purposes and there's no evidence the parent saw the agenda message re: failure

This will be the protocol for each grade reporting period.

Non-Negotiable Protocols for Everyone

From: Kwame Carr
To: Turner Middle
Subject: Non-negotiable Protocols

1. Be sure to attend the CCRPI meeting each month, barring an emergency or a county sponsored meeting, all planned practices for clubs, sports or otherwise, need to be rescheduled on these days, no exceptions - including today

2. Be prepared - having something or nothing to "say" is a strong indication of work ethic in regard to the CCRPI measures and our success as a school - each presentation has a role and ELA/Rdg. and math are no longer the sole measures of school success

3. Each grade level needs designated locker times - twice per day

4. There are no mass restroom breaks @ 6th period

5. There is no lining up to enter classrooms - these students clog the halls during the transition of almost 800 students - devise a plan and let them in

6. Sending students to get a pass because they were tardy has never been our policy since my arrival. Students are moving in the hallways and that's why administrators and teachers man the hallways during each transition. They are typically late because of an adult releasing late or allowing students to complete something in their class. Sending kids back out to get a pass puts more kids back into the hall after the bell, wastes instructional time, causes disorganization, and leads to unmonitored situations. Call the parent of tardy students, use PBIS protocols, assign detention and contact your grade level administrator as a last resort.

7. Release all classes on time - everyone only has 47 minutes to teach - the only option to alleviate that is to take one planning period away from each grade level and expand class time.

8. There is no duty-free lunch at the middle school level in Georgia for teachers with classes during lunch - remain with your classes. Do not rely on the principal, whose schedule is inconsistent, or the assistant principals, who are obligated to manage the other 75% of students that aren't at lunch at any given time. An AP will be in the cafeteria when two are in the building and both are frequently in there at some point during the day.

9. Devise a connections transition plan and stick to it by grade level

10. Contacting parents is in the nature of our job, for good and for bad. Don't allow the failure

notification protocol to change your professionalism!

11. Participate in the school-wide RTI process as outlined, produce data, and provide evidence of your participation and data (content area teachers)

12. Sign in on time - the grace period is rapidly ending for tardy professionals

13. Submit lesson plans each week ahead of time without a reminder - this grace period has closed

14. Follow the curriculum, implement CDAs, their timelines, and expectations, unless told otherwise by the County Level Curriculum Specialists.

15. Follow the school-wide Writing Plan.

None of this is new information; however, the enforcement of these expectations will be applied with renewed enthusiasm to create an awesome learning environment.

Grading Policy Design for ALL Classes

From: Kwame Carr
Sent: Wednesday, June 18, 2014 10:30 AM
To: Turner Middle
Subject: FW: FINAL Grading Guidelines

FYI - Our grading policy is within Douglas County expectations:

- one recorded grade per week must be entered into the online reporting system
- 50% of course grade comes from summative assessments (common assessments, unit assessments, teacher assessments)
- 5% of course grade may be homework (maximum percentage allowable)
- 45% of course grade remains your choice – classwork, projects, portfolios, reports, etc. (choose at least three categories that add to 45%)

| Syllabi/Assessments and Grading – Principal Bradley Model |

From: Kwame Carr
Sent: Tuesday, August 9, 2011 4:28 PM
To: Turner Middle
Subject: Syllabi / Summative Assessments / Formative Assessments - explained in detail

Please **PRINT** and **READ** and **DIGEST** this week and **MAKE ANY NECESSARY CHANGES** to your syllabi **BY FRIDAY, AUGUST 12th**.

I have not presented or taught very well the theory and practical application of the 50% summative assessment grading practice to all faculty and staff. However, I am fortunate to have teachers who have looked at the research, Turner's data, and understand current literature and understand and explain the purpose behind this requirement and what it could do for student achievement in the standards-based classroom. Teacher leaders are essential to school improvement and schools in general. To help everyone, please focus on these talking points when presenting this requirement to students or parents:

1. Rigor is required in the new Georgia Standards and Common Core;
2. Rigor requires the best efforts of teachers and students;
3. Testing requirements exists in Georgia and beyond for various reasons, whether we like them or not;
4. Students are being held to higher expectations by the Georgia Standards;
5. If student lessons are not presented based on Georgia Standards and students are not assessed based on standards, students will not be successful on curriculum-based tests (a real problem at Turner);
6. The data shows that Turner ranks very close to the bottom on all standardized tests—curriculum based and general achievement - when compared to schools within and outside of Douglas County Schools.

While we have shown gains in CRCT achievement, overall we are far behind many schools within the state; The data also shows that students have received fairly good grades on the curriculum without a comparable performance on independent assessments based on the same curriculum delivered in the classroom. A major contributing factor has been the use of many other components to determine grades (which are appropriate) but not enough weight being given to **summative assessments** (that are designed to show how much the student mastered or knows about each standard). There must be a correlation between a standards-based grade and a standards-based state test.

Formative assessments must count very little; they must be designed to help scaffold the student to a higher and deeper level of achievement before the summative assessment is given. For Turner students, formative assessments need to be used as a tool by teachers to get students ready for summative assessments for each standard and/or unit of standards. The formative assessments must show what the student knows or does not know in small bits or chunks. But it also requires the teacher to re-teach using a different strategy or several (differentiated strategies) to help those students who did not get it. Teachers may have several learning groups going on in one class. Teachers may not use a whole group strategy, give a formative assessment, students fail, and the teacher moves on. The teacher must investigate and analyze the formative assessment data and determine what s/he needs to do to scaffold the student up to the class target <u>before giving the summative assessment.</u>

The scaffolding process must include interventions that the teacher must make mandatory and not permissive or voluntary and must occur before the students are given the summative assessment, within reasonable time using your best professional judgment.

Example: Social Studies Class (Assumed Standard): Students must know the history and structure of the branches of government. (Assume this is a Power Standard: lots of questions on the CRCT in social studies— and is deemed very important and assessed in ThinkGate and AIMSweb)

Day 1 - history may be presented in a retrieval chart using the overhead projector, a website on the computer, or playing a game. At the end of the class, students should take a formative assessment (five short questions covering only the significant history presented in the lesson from the overhead, the computer, playing a game, or verbal presentation, et cetera.) The teacher should very quickly tally results to determine the effectiveness of the lesson and give feedback to the students. If 80% (our target) or more of the students made an 85% or higher, consider moving on but also consider the 15% who did not make 85% or higher and determine what you must do to move them forward the next day. (Here: An intervention may be needed for the 15%: after-school tutorial or morning tutorial)

Day 2- At the top of the next day, reinforce the learning by requiring your students to write a paragraph with as many details that they can recall on the following: What are the branches of government and their respective histories? (May be a Do Now for 10 minutes???). Collect this assessment which is really another formative assessment. Now move on to the structure of the branches of government with the 85% that got it and move back to history with 15% that did not get it. Use the essay to see if the 15% has now shown their knowledge in writing. If so, move them on; if not, have a strategy to re-teach history to them. Present appropriate instructional strategies to both groups and assess structure and/or history again focusing on 85% or more. Give feedback to the students.

Day 3 - If knowledge of history and structure is achieved, move on to contemporary issues regarding the branches of government. Recommended Strategy-- maybe an issue search in the media center or an on-line computer search using index cards to gather information both pro and con about the branches of government that could also be used to debate. The students do not literally need to debate, but they must have command of information on both sides of the issue. Of course a spirited debate could be scored using a checklist and rubric.

Day 4 - (an assessment - formative) more feedback to the student.

Day 5-Use instructional strategies in class to reinforce all of the components of the standard(s) to keep retention high among students and to sure-up your struggling students. A review using instructional strategies that require a performance task may be ideal. Students can make a foldable with history on one side, structure in the middle, and pro and con issues and information on the other side.

Day 6—Give a **Summative Assessment** <u>wherein students must answer questions at the level of rigor and cognition required by the CRCT on the standard</u>. Analyze results and give feed back to the student. If you plan to give 10 summative tests, each should count 5% of the overall grade, totaling 50%. The rest of the student's grade is determined by the other components of your grading formula.

YOU HAVE SPENT THE MOST TIME PLANNING WHILE THE STUDENTS SPEND THE MOST TIME LEARNING. Please do no harm by using the 50% summative assessment requirement to fail students, when in actuality the 50% is really designed to help improve student achievement, learning in general, as well as our standardized test scores. Teachers are in no way exempt from meeting all of the usual requirements before failing a student and must very carefully use formative assessments to build students up to summative assessments. This must work in favor of the students, not against them.

Syllabus Example:

50% Summative Assessments --> please do not include <u>any</u> other descriptor on this line other than "summative assessments" - this line is mandatory

30% Classwork

10% Project

05% Homework (this is the max percentage allowable)

05% Notebook

Laptop Security

From: Kwame Carr
Sent: Saturday, April 20, 2013 7:21 AM
To: Turner Middle
Subject: FW: lap top security

Additionally, whether this is the case or not, please remember the expectation of securing laptops overnight. As I inspect the building at some point over the course of most weekends, several people have become too comfortable leaving laptops in their rooms in clear view, unlocked, mainly on docking stations. We have many weekend activities and people access the building during non-school hours. We've also had three incidences where exterior doors have been mistakenly left open or ajar over the weekend. Please eliminate unnecessary losses by being proactive and not reactive in the event such mistakes lead to missing equipment. Thank you!

From: James

Date: Fri, 19 Apr 2013 16:09:22 -0400

To: Turner Middle<Turner.Middle@douglas.k12.ga.us>

Subject: lap top security

The other day I heard a student telling another student about our secret username/password to use our laptops at home. This student knew the username and password. <u>Please be reminded that students should under **NO** circumstance be told the username or password to our laptops.</u> If you have children at this school and you have given the home user information to them, please take time this weekend to remind them that they should not be sharing that information with other students (I'm not insinuating they have, just taking precautions).

Principle 5 – School Improvement

School Improvement Plan

School Name: Turner Middle School 2014-2015

Planning Committee Members:

NAME	POSITION/ROLE
Kwame Carr	Principal
John	Assistant Principal
Dr. Carol	Instructional Lead Teacher
Jamie	Math Teacher
Sarah	Assistant Principal
Sheliah	Parent/PTA/Paraprofessional

*1. A comprehensive needs assessment of the entire school that addresses all academic areas and other factors that may affect achievement.

Response:

A. We have developed our school-wide plan with the participation of individuals who will carry out the comprehensive school-wide/school improvement program plan. Those persons involved were Kwame Carr, John, Dr. Carol, Jamie, Sarah, Sheliah. The ways they were involved were by analyzing school-wide achievement data and providing strategies to address deficits in student achievement as well as ways to allocate resources.
B. We have used the following instruments, procedures, or processes to obtain this information: CRCT data analysis along with CDA reviews; identification of strengths and weaknesses based upon student achievement data; recommendation of research based strategies to address these deficits in student achievement.
C. We have taken into account the needs of migrant children by (or if you have no migratory students . . . these are the procedures we would follow should those students be in attendance: We will administer pre-assessments to migrant children to determine their academic needs and design individualized programs to address academic deficits. This includes incorporation of the RTI process and possible placement in our FLP.
D. We have reflected current achievement data that will help the school understand the subjects and skills in which teaching and learning need to be improved. For example, students with disabilities and our English language learners currently have deficiencies in science and social studies due to their deficits in vocabulary comprehension.
E. We have based our plan on information about all students in the school and identified students and groups of students who are not yet achieving to the State Academic content standards [the Common Core Georgia Performance Standards (CCGPS)] and the State student academic achievement standards including
    - Economically disadvantaged students . . .
    - Students with Disabilities
    - Students with limited English proficiency . . .
F. The data has helped us reach <u>conclusions</u> regarding achievement or other related data.
    - The major <u>strengths</u> we found in our program were . . .
    Reading with Fluency and Comprehension, Mathematics – algebra and measurement, ELA and Writing – conventions and style

    - The major <u>needs</u> we discovered were science, social studies, the geometry and data analysis strands in mathematics, and writing among SWD and ELL students
    - The <u>needs we will address</u> are science, social studies, math and writing among SWD and ELL students
    - The <u>specific academic needs</u> of those students that are to be addressed in the schoolwide program plan will be vocabulary, flexible (small) grouping, and the writing process
        o The ROOTCAUSE that we discovered for each of the needs was an <u>emphasis of resources have been traditionally geared towards other content; science and social studies were not an equal indicator of student achievement using AYP; basic proficiency in math, reading, and ELA have been the target.</u>

*1. A comprehensive needs assessment of the entire school that addresses all academic areas and other factors that may affect achievement.
G. The measurable <u>goals/benchmarks</u> we have established to address the needs were pre, interim, post teacher assessment data, CDA district-wide data, SLO (student learning objective) data, CRCT data and targets, and Milestone data and targets.

*2. School-wide reform strategies that are scientifically researched based, directly tied to the comprehensive needs assessment and academic standards.
Response: - Identification of our Student Focus Groups using Economically Disadvantaged achievement data, SWD achievement data, and ELL achievement data - Implementation of RTI Process to remediate students not meeting standards - Implementation of our Flexible Learning Program for students not meeting standards - Implementation of our after school tutoring program to provide extra learning time - Initiate flexible (small) grouping to provide students additional, personalized, differentiated instruction

2(a). School-wide reform strategies that provide opportunities for all children in the school to meet or exceed Georgia's proficient and advanced levels of student performance.
A. *Response:* The ways in which we will address the needs of all children in the school particularly the needs of students furthest away from demonstrating proficiency related to the State's academic content and student academic achievement standard are: - Interpreting and analyzing school-wide assessment data (e.g., ELA, Math, Science, Social Studies CDAs, periodic writing assessments, SLDS data, and SLO data), providing flexible (small) grouping and differentiating instruction based upon results. - Providing planning times/days and adequate time for collaboration - Continuing to implement and refine Standards-Based Classroom components in all classrooms, incorporating the Learning Focused Schools model. - Continuing to implement and broaden the use of PD360 and increasing student achievement in all classrooms and content areas. - Continuing to implement writing across the curriculum. - Providing differentiated instruction for students participating in Special Education classes and English Language Learner Programs (ESOL). - Utilizing co-teaching and inclusion models of instruction for students with disabilities, ELL students, and IEP students. - Providing before and after school instruction to preview and reinforce the curriculum – Implementation of a Flexible Learning Program afterschool - Incorporating use of technology (Promethean Boards, United Streaming, Odyssey, Active Slates, etc.) during instruction. - Utilizing literature circles, reading and writing workshops for implementation of reading/language arts standards. - Utilizing non-fiction selections (such as leveled readers and other high interest sources) for teaching reading/language arts standards. - Utilizing programs and resources for specific student needs such as: System 44, Leveled Reading Library, 25 Book Campaign, Academic Mondays and remediation and enrichment for all content areas facilitated by instructional personnel thru Response to Intervention - Incorporating project-based and cooperative learning strategies in classrooms.

2(a). School-wide reform strategies that provide opportunities for all children in the school to meet or exceed Georgia's proficient and advanced levels of student performance.

- Continuing to refine goal setting (SMART goals) and monitoring/graphing results by students, applying Response to Intervention strategies
- Reinforcing effort and recognizing achievement in classrooms, on bulletin boards, during school-wide assemblies, and in parent communications.
- Posting resources on the shared school server which allows quick access for the Professional Learning Communities.
- Planning and implementing Family Nights for the purpose of informing parents of ways to reinforce academic skills.
- Communicating to students and parents through school newsletters, school websites, agendas, Parent Teacher Association (PTA) meetings, School Council, ParentLink, and the School Social Worker.
- Incorporation of iPass software to remediate and accelerate students in math during our Flexible Learning Program
- Replenishing disposable equipment required for successful implementation of programs such as Read 180 and minicomputers such as NetBooks (e.g. Head phones with speaking & listening capabilities)
- Using BrainPop software to remediate students
- Implementing Study Island to monitor, remediate, and accelerate students in the areas of Science and Math
- Utilize Word Games to assist in vocabulary development – e.g. Scrabble,
- Securing consultants as professional developers for our faculty in the implementation of best practices in differentiation and relationship building

2(b). Are based upon effective means of raising student achievement.

A. *Response:* Following (or in our appendices) are examples of the SCIENTIFICALLY BASED RESEARCH supporting our effective methods and instructional practices or strategies. . Learning Focused Schools Framework by Dr. Max Thompson, Response to Intervention, ThinkGate, AimsWeb, Teacher Keys Evaluation System (State of Georgia), Read 180, iPass, Study Island, OAS, Odyssey, System 44, iLearn, Mathline, Dr. Marzano's High Impact Rubric, and Dr. Thomas Murphy's achievement gap strategies are scientifically based instructional practices supporting student achievement.

2(c). Use effective instructional methods that increase the quality and amount of learning time.

B. *Response:* We will <u>increase</u> the amount and <u>quality</u> of learning time by:
- Providing a **Flexible Learning Program (FLP)** as a Connections Reading Class infused with science and social studies vocabulary and content
- Creating an RTI process for science, social studies, math, and writing for targeted students needing additional assistance in grades 6-8 using the Online Assessment System Formative Assessment Bank, the instructional lead teacher, and teachers during the school day

2(c). Use effective instructional methods that increase the quality and amount of learning time.

- Providing tutors for students needing additional assistance in science, social studies, and math thru our after school tutoring program
- Utilizing small-group instruction based upon academic needs of our **Focus School** and using this research-based strategy to close the achievement gap identified by the GaDOE

2(d). Address the needs of all children, particularly targeted populations, and address how the school will determine if such needs have been met and are consistent with improvement plans approved under the Elementary and Secondary Education Act of 1965 (ESEA).

Response: Teachers use data from state tests, system tests, common teacher assessments as well as Learning Focused Schools generated assessments to prepare lesson plans and classroom grouping for understanding of standards. Formative assessments are used to check for understanding of the Essential Question and standard(s) being taught that day, before students depart the classroom. Formative and summative assessments are consistently given to check for mastery along the way and upon completion of teaching a unit. The level of mastery dictates the amount of re-teaching that continues in the next unit.

Administrators assist teachers with the disaggregation of local, state, and system assessment data. Teachers are provided the breakdown of these data to determine if acceleration or re-teaching is required. This data is vital to teachers in preparation of their lessons to provide differentiation to their students; sometimes this means pulling students for a short period of time from non-academic classes or pull out from the same subject area to combine similar learning styles.

2(e). Must include documentation to support that any educational field trip used as an instructional strategy is aligned to the comprehensive needs assessment found in the school-wide plan and must be connected to the support of assisting students to achieve proficiency or advanced status in relation to the State Academic content standards. Documentation must be provided during the budget approval process. Required based on FY12 US ED monitoring.

Response: We do not take educational field trips with our Title I funds.

*3.   Instruction by highly qualified professional staff.

Response: Instruction at Turner Middle School is provided by highly qualified teachers and supported by paraprofessionals who meet the requirements of "highly qualified' as defined by Title 1 and the EASA Waiver. Each year teacher certification and teaching assignments are reviewed to ensure that teachers are highly qualified under both Title I and the standards established by the State of Georgia. Teachers and paraprofessionals are reminded of renewal dates, procedures, and required coursework, if needed, to renew their certification. If any teacher is out of field, teaching assignments are changed to meet compliance.

Staff members who have to be out for long-term leave (e.g., maternity leave) will have their positions filled by substitutes who are certified teachers in the required content area. This fulfills the highly qualified requirement. If at some point a regular staff member or substitute is not highly qualified, parent letters are sent notifying parents of the status of that teacher.

*3(a).   Strategies to attract highly qualified teachers to high-needs schools.

A.   *Response:* We will provide instruction by highly qualified teachers who meet the standards established by the state of Georgia. (Use HiQ Report and school staff roster. Indicate how certification deficiencies are being addressed.)

*4.   Professional development for staff to enable all children in the school

Response:

A.   We have included teachers, principals, paraprofessionals and, if appropriate, service personnel, parents, and other staff in our staff development that addresses the root causes of our identified needs. For example, staff members analyzed norm-referenced and criterion-referenced test results as well as other student assessments and surveys to determine the strengths and weaknesses of the school to plan for professional development.

B.   We have aligned professional development with the State's academic content and student academic achievement standards by selecting professional development that correlates with data deficits in our student achievement measures, especially among our focus students; for example, vocabulary training for our ELL population in science and social studies

*4. Professional development for staff to enable all children in the school

C. We have devoted sufficient monetary funds, an instructional lead teacher (ILT), and an additional planning period for teachers to effectively carry out the <u>professional development activities that address the root causes</u> of academic problems.

D. We have included teachers in professional development activities regarding the use of academic assessments to enable them to provide information on, and to improve, the achievement of individual students and the overall instructional program in the following ways: Weekly, all staff members (certified) are engaged in professional learning opportunities. Monthly, each Professional Learning Community analyzes, reviews, and revises its school improvement plan using a Short-term Action Plan (SAP). Strategies that have been successful for each team are shared through the CCRPI Leadership Team and thus the school. Some of the actions completed by groups are as follows:

- Developing assessment tools
- Identifying strategies/materials to address needs
- Planning lessons to implement the strategies w/materials
- Developing/designing materials to address needs
- Demonstrating/practicing strategies members have used or will use
- Examining samples of student work for evidence of student understanding
- Assessing results after using strategies in classrooms
- Visiting each other's classrooms to observe strategies in action
- Researching additional proven strategies

Academic Assessment data is reviewed and discussed by the Leadership Team and brought before the whole faculty to identify areas of strengths and weaknesses for all subgroups at Turner Middle School.

*5. Strategies to increase parental involvement.

Response:

We have involved parents in the planning, review, and improvement of the comprehensive school-wide program plan by: Parents have been involved in the planning, review, and improvement of the comprehensive school-wide plan by participation in the needs assessment and surveys. Parents are also part of the Parent Advisory Council. Parents play a valuable role in reviewing data, planning, and designing the school-wide plan. We also offer various Parent Workshops. The improvement plan is available for all parents to review via the school website.

We have provided written notice to parents of each of our enrolled students that we have been identified as a "**Focus School**," in a format, and to the extent practical, in a language that the parent can understand.

- A. We have developed a parent involvement policy included in our appendices that
  - ➢ includes strategies to increase parental involvement (such as family literacy services)
  - ➢ describes how the school will provide individual student academic assessment results, including a interpretation of those results
  - ➢ makes the comprehensive school-wide program plan available to the LEA, parents, and the public (internet, newspaper, newsletters)
  - ➢ compacts required – include with policy
  - ➢ Parent Involvement checklist included

*6. Plans for assisting in the transition from elementary programs to middle school programs.

Response:

- A. Following are our plans for assisting elementary children in the transition from elementary programs. Also included are transition plans for students entering **middle school** and entering from private schools plus students entering our school throughout the school year.
- Visits to elementary schools by Peer Mediators, band students, and counselors.
- Monthly orientation for newly enrolled students by peer mediators and student ambassadors
- Buddy Program, which is a student lead advisory program. Middle school students partner with elementary students to help ease the anxiety of transitioning to middle school.
- Elementary School tours in May to acclimate elementary students to Turner Middle School.

*7. Measures to include teachers in the decisions regarding the use of assessment to provide information on, and to improve, the performance of individual students and the overall instructional program.

Response:

A. The ways that we include teachers in decisions regarding use of academic assessment are: Teachers use data from State assessments, system assessments, common teacher assessments as well as Learning Focused Schools generated assessments to prepare lesson plans and classroom grouping for understanding of standards. Formative assessments are used to check for understanding of the Essential Question, standard(s) being taught that day, before students depart the classroom. Unit assessments and quizzes are given to check for mastery along the way or upon completion of teaching a unit. The level of mastery dictates the amount of re-teaching that continues in the next unit.

Administrators assist teachers with the disaggregation of state and system testing data. Teachers are provided the breakdown of these data to determine if acceleration or re-teaching is required. This data is vital to teachers in preparation of their lessons to provide differentiation to their students; sometimes this means pulling students for a short period of time from non-academic classes or pull out from the same subject area to combine similar learning styles

*8. Coordination and integration of Federal, State, and local services and programs.

Response:

Turner Middle School offers CHAMP after school services to any qualified students and also offers free **FLP** services to all qualifying, tiered students through a connections class during the regular school day.

Use of Title I funds will provide extended tutoring assistance to students during the school day, after school, on some Saturdays, and during summer school and will also provide the needed resources to address students' learning deficiencies and address their learning styles.

Instructional Lead Teacher (ILT)

A. An academic lead teacher is employed at Turner Middle School to provide professional development in our areas of need, specifically, ongoing training in differentiation techniques, applications of universal design, and the implementation of Learning Focus Schools. We currently emphasize social studies, science, and mathematics; however, we will continue to monitor our need for other content areas. The ILT is responsible for ensuring student excitement, engagement and comprehension of core content and often provides students with pull-out opportunities to ensure content mastery.

8(a). List of State and local educational agency programs and other federal programs that will be included.

Response: Title 1 Funds, 21st Century Grant - CHAMP, School Improvement Funds, Flexible Learning Program Funds

8(b). Description of how resources from Title I and other sources will be used.

Response: Based upon our Focus School status we will continue to provide our students with additional resources in science and social studies. Although our current achievement gap is between our White and Special Education population, it is necessary to ensure the resources provided are allocated to our school-wide Title 1 program to eliminate the potential of becoming a Focus, Priority, or Alert school due to any other subgroup. Since we have also had documented achievement gaps in mathematics, we deem it necessary to provide additional resources in this content area as well.

Funds will be allocated to our Flexible Learning Program, our After School Tutoring Program, Professional Development, Summer School, our Instructional Lead Teacher, our Parent Outreach Facilitator, and to the reduction of class sizes in science and social studies which has been scientifically researched as an effective means to decrease the achievement gap.

8(c). Plan developed in coordination with other programs, including those under the School-to-Work Opportunities Act of 1994, the Carl D. Perkins Vocational and Applied Technology Act, and National and Community Service Act of 1990.

Response: The plan was developed in coordination with other programs, including those under the School-to-Work Opportunities Act of 1994, the Carl D. Perkins Vocational and Applied Technology Act, and National and Community Service Act of 1990.

*9. Activities to ensure that students who experience difficulty mastering standards shall be provided with effective, timely assistance, which shall include:

Response:

A. We are providing activities to ensure that students who experience difficulty mastering proficient or advanced levels of academic achievement standards shall be provided with effective, timely additional assistance. Those activities are:
- **FLP (Flexible Learning Program)**
- RTI (Response to Intervention)
- SST (Student Support Team)
- After school Tutoring Program

9(a). Measures to ensure that student weaknesses are identified on a timely basis.

Response: **FLP**, RTI, and SST programs which are designed to identify and monitor student with learning difficulties. Subject area benchmarks provide indicators of student strengths and weaknesses. Individual writing folders are kept for each student from elementary to middle school. These folders show teachers and students evidence of developmental progress. Weekly conference times are available for teachers and parents to discuss students' academic and behavioral issues. Half days are scheduled each semester to provide extra time for teacher-parent communication and for professional development of teachers. The school also provides opportunities for A.M. and after school tutoring.

9(b). Periodic training for teachers in the identification of weaknesses and appropriate assistance for identified weaknesses.

Response: Periodic training will be provided to teachers reinforcing methods and strategies for the identification of difficulties and appropriate methods of assistance for these difficulties:

- Training for Writing Assessments
- Milestone training
- RTI Training
- SST training, professional development
- Teacher Keys training
- Learning-Focused Schools training

9c). Teacher-parent conferences that detail what the school will do to help the student, what the parents can do to help the student, and additional assistance available to the student at the school or n the community.

Response: We will hold teacher –parent conferences that detail what the school will do to help the student, what the parents can do to help the students and additional assistance available to the student at the school or in the community.

- PTSA meetings
- **FLP** Saturday tutoring/meetings/workshops
- CHAMP
- Parent Nights
- Parent Luncheons - Invite parents to eat lunch with their child

Parent conferences held on half-day/early release days (September 2014 and March 2015)

10. Description of how individual student assessment results and interpretation will be provided to parents.

Response: The Georgia Department of Education provides detailed information for interpreting CRCT/**Milestones** test scores and the Middle Grades Writing Assessment (to be discontinued). The World-Class Instructional Design and Assessment (WIDA) provides detailed information about ACCESS testing procedures and score interpretation. ESOL teachers are trained and tested before giving the ACCESS test to their students. Teachers provide rubrics to explain the grading process for some assessments outside of standardized testing and assessment. Parents are provided the same information, either before a test is given, or a copy is provided along with the test results, as deemed appropriate.

11. Provisions for the collection and disaggregation of data on the achievement and assessment results of students.
Response: As state achievement test results are received by the Principal and the testing coordinator, all concerned parties receive a breakdown by school, grade level teacher and subject area by grade level. Interpretations are provided as well as comparisons within the school and district. This data is provided in a timely manner in order to allow for remediation and promotion/placement/retention decisions concerning students and for communication of such decisions with students and parents/guardians. Individual teacher assessments are scored and feedback is given to the students in a timely manner in order to allow for remediation and/or acceleration as directed by the student's mastery level.
12. Provisions to ensure that disaggregated assessment results for each category are valid and reliable.
Response: Leadership team(s) will develop reporting protocols for each category as results are received. Each department will meet to develop strategies for implementation and completion. The principal will require each teacher to submit their individual assessment data for all students taught during the course of an academic year.

13. Provisions for public reporting of disaggregated data.
Response: The report will be published on the school website. A copy of the report will be available in the front office for public viewing and in the principal's office.

14. Plan developed during a one-year period, unless LEA, after considering the recommendation of its technical assistance providers, determines that less time is needed to develop and implement the school-wide program.
Response: Our plan is revised each school year

15. Plan developed with the involvement of the community to be served and individuals who will carry out the plan including teachers, principals, other school staff, and pupil service personnel, parents and students (if secondary).
Response: Our community stakeholders include faculty, the leadership team, local school council, parent advisory committee and our Parent Teacher Student Association

16. Plan available to the LEA, parents, and the public.	
Response: All documentation, including the Title 1 Plan, has been written in languages relevant to the student population. They are also available online. A translator is available / present at all parent workshops, when appropriate.	
17. Plan translated to the extent feasible, into any language that a significant percentage of the parents of participating students in the school speak as their primary language.	
Response: Our School Improvement Plan is translated, to the extent feasible, into any language that a significant percentage of the parents of participating students in the school speak as their primary language.	
18. Plan is subject to the school improvement provisions of Section 1116.	
Response: The plan is subject to the school improvement provisions of section 1116.	

Budget Aligned to School Improvement Plan

Title I Budget Detail Plan

Amendment # APPLICATION
Budget Change # 0

$ 451,675

All budgeted funds must be in whole dollars.

1000 Instructional Services

Object	Cost per person	Description		Projected Cost
5110	Grade	Teacher Salary *(enter name)*	Subject	
	6	*John*	*Social Studies*	$ 50,000
	6	*Jane*	*Science*	$ 42,000
	6,7,8	*Doe*	*Math*	$ 67,000
		Total Salaries:	$ 159,000	
5113	$64/day	SALARIES -SUBS FOR TI TCHRS		$ 960
5140		SALARIES -AIDES/PARAPRO		
5199		SALARIES -TUTOR/SUMMER SCH		$ 43,000
521010	$11,340/yr	GROUP HEALTH - TEACHERS	0	$ -
522010	6.20%	FICA - TEACHERS		$ 9,858
522110	1.45%	MEDICARE -TEACHERS		$ 2,306
522013	6.2%	FICA -SUBSTITUTES		$ 60
522113	1.45%	MEDICARE -SUBSTITUTES		$ 14
522040	6.2%	FICA -AIDES/PARAPROS		$ -
522140	1.45%	MEDICARE -AIDES/PARAPROS		$ -
522099	6.20%	FICA -TUTOR/SUMMER SCH		$ 2,666
522199	1.45%	MEDICARE - TUTOR/SUMMER SCH		$ 624
523010	13.15%	TRS - TEACHERS		$ 20,909
525010	$25 ea.	UNEMPLOYMENT-TEACHERS	0	$ -
526010	0.75%	WORKERS COMP- TEACHERS		$ 1,193

15,526

	529010	$17/mo	VISION, DENTAL, LIFE-TCHRS	0	$ -
	530080		PURCHASED SERVICES (*OUTSIDE INSTRUCTORS*)		
	5610		SUPPLIES		$ 10,000
	5611		TECHNOLOGY SUPPLIES		
	5612		SOFTWARE		$ 35,000
	5615		EXPENDABLE EQUIPMENT (*OVER $50*)		
	5616		EXPENDABLE COMPUTER EQUIPMENT (*OVER $50*)		
	5642		BOOK AND PERIODICALS (*NO TEXTBKS/LIBRARY BOOKS*)		$ 1,000
	Total				$ 286,587

2210 Professional Development

	Object	Cost per person	Description		Projected Cost
	5113	$64 day/LT $88	SALARIES -SUBSTITUTES FOR CERTIFIED STAFF		$ 3,456
	5116		SALARIES -STIPENDS/HONORARIUMS		
	5191		OTHR SALARIES EMPLOYEE CONSULT		$ 5,000
	5191		SALARIES- ILT	Subject	
			Jean	*ILT*	$ 74,000
	521091	$11,340/yr	GROUP HEALTH - ILT	0	$ -
6,308	522013	6.2%	FICA -SUBSTITUTES		$ 214
	522113	1.45%	MEDICARE -SUBSTITUTES		$ 50
	522016	6.2%	FICA -STIPENDS/HONORARIUMS		$ -
	522116	1.45%	MEDICARE -STIPENDS/HONORARIUMS		$ -
	522091	6.2%	FICA -OTHR SALARIES/ILT		$ 4,898
	522191	1.45%	MEDICARE -OTHER SALARIES/ILT		$ 1,146
	523091	13.15%	TRS - ILT's		$ 9,731
	525091	$25 ea.	UNEMPLOYMENT-ILT	0	$ -
	526091	0.75%	WORKERS COMP ILT		$ 555

	529091	$17/mo	VISION, DENTAL, LIFE- ILT	0	$ -
	530080		PURCHASED SERVICES (OUTSIDE INSTRUCTORS)		
	5580	.565/mile	TRAVEL FOR EMPLOYEES (EXPENSE REPORT)		$ 12,000
	5610		SUPPLIES		$ 1,500
	5611		TECHNOLOGY SUPPLIES		$ 1,500
	5612		SOFTWARE		
	5615		EXPENDABLE EQUIPMENT (OVER $50)		
	5616		EXPENDABLE COMPUTER EQUIPMENT (OVER $50)		
	5642		BOOK AND PERIODICALS (NO TEXTBKS/LIBRARY BOOKS)		
	5810		DUES AND FEES (REGISTRATION, MEMBERSHIP)		$ 500
			Total		$ 114,550

2600 Maintenance & Operations (Custodial Supplies for Summer School Only)

Object	Cost per person	Description	Projected Cost
5610		SUPPLIES FOR SUMMER SCHOOL -CUSTODIAL	$ 600
Total			$ 600

2700 Student Transportation

	Object	Cost per person	Description	Projected Cost
	5180		SALARIES BUS DRIVERS -SUM SCH/AFTER SCH	$ 12,000
918	522080	6.2%	FICA	$ 744
	522180	1.45%	MEDICARE	$ 174
	562020	$3 per mile	FUEL -SUMMER SCHOOL & AFTER SCHOOL	$ 9,005
	Total			$ 21,923

2900	Parent Engagement Activities				
	Object	Cost per person	Description		Projected Cost
1,683	5140		SALARIES -AIDES/PARAPROS *(CHILDCARE)*		
	5177		SALARIES -ESOL PARENT TUTORING BY EMPLOYEE		
	5177		SALARIES -POF	*Jack*	$ 22,000
	521077	$7,154/yr	GROUP HEALTH - POF		$ -
	522040	6.2%	FICA -AIDES/PARAPROS		$ -
	522140	1.45%	MEDICARE - AIDES/PARAPROS		$ -
	522077	6.2%	FICA -POF/ ESOL TUTORING		$ 1,364
	522177	1.45%	MEDICARE - POF/ESOL TUTORINGS		$ 319
	523077	13.15%	TRS - POF		$ 2,893
	525077	$25 ea.	UNEMPLOYMENT		$ -
	526077	0.75%	WORKERS COMP		$ 165
	529077	$16.56/mo	VISION/DENTAL/LIFE *(Enter Name Below)*		$ -
	530017		PURCHASED SERVICES *(OUTSIDE INTERPRETER)*		
	530019		PURCHASED SERVICES *(OUTSIDE TRANSLATORS)*		$ 200
	530080		PURCHASED SERVICES *(OUTSIDE INSTRUCTORS)*		
	5530		COMMUNICATION *(POSTAGE FOR MAILOUTS)*		
	5580	.565/mile	TRAVEL POF		$ 500
	5610		SUPPLIES		$ 374
	5611		TECHNOLOGY SUPPLIES		$ 200
	5612		SOFTWARE		
	5615		EXPENDABLE EQUIPMENT *(OVER $50)*		
	5616		EXPENDABLE COMPUTER EQUIPMENT *(OVER $50)*		
	5642		BOOK AND PERIODICALS *(NO TEXTBKS/LIBRARY BOOKS)*		
	5810		DUES AND FEES *(REGISTRATION, MEMBERSHIP)*		
	Total				$ 28,015

TOTAL FUNDS ALLOCATED		$ 451,675
BALANCE OF FUNDS TO ALLOCATE (THIS MUST BE "0")	⇨⇨⇨⇨	$ (0)

Participants Who Helped <u>Develop</u> the Plan and <u>Will Assist</u> in Monitoring Its Implementation

Greatest Needs

School: **Turner Middle School**   School Year: **2014 – 2015**

Title I Schools are required to conduct a needs assessment to determine the greatest academic need for students and staff. Title I funds can only be used to support purchases identified in your needs assessment and to support the students who are most in need of academic support. **Please indicate below the greatest area of need in prioritize order based on the analysis of your school's data.**

Prioritized Area of Need

#1 Academic Priority - Subject: **Social Studies**

Strategies for improvement	Materials, supplies and/or services needed
Flexible (small) Groups	Additional Teacher
Provide additional instruction	Flexible Learning Program
Pre-teach vocabulary	Flexible Learning Program
RTI Implementation	Teacher Intervention
Professional Learning	Assessment Writing
Professional Learning	Teaching Strategies for SWD and ELL
Technology needs	Not applicable

#2 Academic Priority - Subject: **Science**

Strategies for improvement	Materials, supplies and/or services needed
Flexible (small) Groups	Additional Teacher
Provide additional instruction	Flexible Learning Program
Pre-teach vocabulary	Flexible Learning Program
RTI Implementation	Teacher Intervention
Professional Learning	Assessment Writing
Professional Learning	Teaching Strategies for SWD and ELL
Technology needs	Not applicable

#3 Academic Priority - Subject: **Mathematics**

Strategies for improvement	Materials, supplies and/or services needed
Flexible (small) Groups	Additional Teacher
RTI Implementation	Teacher Intervention
Professional Learning	Assessment Writing
Professional Learning	Teaching Strategies for SWD and ELL
Technology needs	Not applicable

Needs Assessment

Major Strengths

Strengths	Data and Source
Reading all students	98% CRCT, CDAs, AimsWeb
ELA all students	93% CRCT, CDAs
Math all students	85% CRCT
Writing all students	85% Ga. Middle Grades Assess.

Major Needs (weaknesses)

Need	Data and Source
Science – all students	75% CRCT
Science – SWD	39% CRCT
Social Studies – all students	76% CRCT
Social Studies – SWD	42% CRCT
Writing - SWD	44% MGWA

Needs to Address

Need(s) school will address	Specific academic needs (Be specific about what area needs addressing)
Science – all subgroups	Vocabulary of standards
Science – SWD and ELL	Vocabulary of standards
Social Stud. – all sub groups	Vocabulary of standards
Social Stud. – SWD and ELL	Vocabulary of standards
Writing - SWD	Understanding Writing Pro.

Root Cause Analysis

Need #1

- Why are students not performing well in Science Vocabulary (identified specific academic need)?
    - Answer <u>Emphasis and resources have been traditionally geared towards other content</u>
        - Why? <u>Science was not an equal indicator of student achievement using AYP</u>
            - Why? <u>Basic proficiency in math, reading, and ELA have been the target</u>
                - Why? <u>Science vocabulary has not been an explicit focus</u>

Need #2

- Why are students not performing well in Social Stud. Vocabulary (identified specific academic need)?
    - Answer <u>Emphasis and resources have been traditionally geared towards other content</u>
        - Why? <u>Social Studies was not an equal indicator of student achievement using AYP</u>
            - Why? <u>Basic proficiency in math, reading, and ELA have been the target</u>
                - Why? <u>Social Studies vocabulary has not been an explicit focus</u>

Need #3

- Why are students not performing well in Writing (identified specific academic need)?
    - Answer <u>Students (SWD) have not been expected to write across curriculum and across grade levels</u>
        - Why? <u>Writing was primarily addressed in grade eight</u>

            Why? <u>8th graders were the only grade assessed on Ga. Writing Test</u>

Narrative of Needs

Title 1 Narrative to Support Allocation of Teacher Funding to Reduce Class Size

(...in science and social studies)

Turner Middle School has been designated as a Focus School based upon achievement data during the 2011 spring administration of the CRCT. A Focus School is identified by the achievement gap measurement between the highest performing subgroup and the lowest performing subgroup in specific content areas. Our achievement gap has been identified in the areas of science and social studies among our white student population and our students with disabilities.

Research conducted on achievement gaps among students strongly suggests that several factors can be manipulated to effectively close the gap. The two most effective strategies have been found to be effective teachers and classroom management (Marzano 2003, What Works in Schools). Another identified correlate of student achievement among all subgroups is the amount of one on one attention students receive during instruction on a regular basis. Dr. Thomas Murphy (Closing the Achievement Gap, 2007) has found class size to be a factor. Reducing class size allows students to have more individualized attention and instruction.

Closing the achievement gap requires students to receive more individualized instruction. Time constraints often occur with larger classes, hence students' inability to receive such attention. Teachers are better able to serve smaller, struggling classes and help students fill in their gaps in learning when the student to teacher ratio is smaller.

Principle 6 – RTI (Response to Intervention esp. SWD & ELL)

RTI Protocol

1. Identify students that failed a portion of the CRCT and/or are special ed. - **this is a pre-planning expectation**
2. Construct a working framework to pull students during planning time
3. Graph your information

Prepare evidence and a 3-minute faculty presentation (no PowerPoint, Prezi or technology required) each month; name the students you've met to remediate during your planning, and summarize your plan of action and its effectiveness during the last RTI cycle

RTI Article by Educator David Beall

At Turner Middle School we proudly say that we are "the best middle school in Georgia." It is not just a claim, but a mindset, where excellence is expected on a daily basis from the faculty, students, staff and administration. We give ourselves this challenge in order to push our students to be the best students they can be. They deserve no less in order to prepare for a highly competitive world. Knowledge and learning will translate into achievement and career success after our students leave us for high school, college and the post-graduate world. One tool that we have used to further our students' academic success is the RTI or Response to Intervention process. This tiered approach to helping students catch up with their same-age peers in skills they may be lacking is one reason that TMS has been so competitive when it comes to test scores.

The process is fairly simple. All students begin on Tier 1; receiving the kind of standards-based instruction that all students in Georgia receive each year. Then, as data is collected through formative assessments, students are identified for more intensive interventions on Tiers 2 and 3. Students are given extra skills and knowledge instruction weekly in subjects where they may be struggling. All faculty members at Turner identify students who are struggling in the subjects that they teach and pull them aside weekly for additional instruction during their planning time. What makes the process unique at Turner is that students with disabilities are also given additional support above and beyond the requirements of their IEPs to help them succeed at a rate similar to their non-disabled peers. This additional support is crucial to helping our students with disabilities access the curriculum.

Our principal, Kwame Carr, made student achievement his top priority upon taking the helm of Turner Middle School in 2011. In the brief three-year span since then, we have made significant gains in student achievement, as indicated by our test score data. For example, between the years 2011-2014, Turner Middle School saw increases in the percentage of students passing the CRCT in all academic areas. The largest increases were in science and social studies, with a 12% percent gain in science achievement and a 23% percent gain in social studies. Among students with disabilities, the data shows a tremendous difference between the baseline year of 2011 and the most recent data from spring of 2014. The passing rates increased by 26% in language arts, 37% in math, 21% in reading, 10% in science and 32% in social studies.

Granted, we are proud of the achievements of our students and teachers here at Turner. However, with the new Georgia Milestones Test assessing our students and teachers on a student growth model, there is no time to rest on our laurels. We will continue to provide standards-based instruction and extra support to any student who requires that extra push to succeed. We know that when our students succeed, our community succeeds as well. These students are our future business leaders, civil servants, entrepreneurs, inventors, scientists, and teachers. Our very future will be determined by how well we serve them. At Turner, we feel honored and privileged to be chosen for this important task.

Strategies for School Improvement

In the area of Curriculum Implementation and Understanding the Common Core:

Content area teachers and instructional leaders study the Georgia Standards in collaborative groups in order to know the concepts and skills required in the standards and elements and become familiar with vertical standards and elements.

Faculty and administration study the CC/GPS to understand the rigor and performance required through the language of the standards to reach consensus on mastery of the standards and develop sample performance tasks.

Faculty and administration outline topics for professional learning that will be needed by teachers to strengthen instruction for challenging standards.

School leadership provides staff with current research and samples of various curriculum maps and units. Discussions are held to clarify the purpose and expected use of the curriculum maps and units prior to beginning any curriculum development.

Teachers participate in developing curriculum maps that provide the sequence of concepts, standards, and skills, and the time periods for teaching the content. Designated check points using performance tasks, formative and summative assessments are made clear. A scope and sequence process or checklist is used to ensure that every element and standard will have designated instructional times within the maps.

Various templates utilizing a design for unit development are reviewed and teachers collaboratively select a template for use. Template designs include, but are not limited to examples from McTighe and Wiggins, Understanding by Design, Ainsworth's, Power Standards, etc. The Georgia Department of Education's Curriculum Framework is an example of units utilizing a common design.

The teachers and administrators study the vertical and horizontal scope of the standards to ensure appropriate instruction for a grade or subject. To prepare for a vertical alignment, teachers review standards in the previous grade level to understand what students have been taught the year before. They also review the standards of the next grade level to understand what is expected the following year. Secondary teachers review the standards of prerequisite and subsequent subject areas.

Teachers and other instructional leaders align the state curriculum (CC/GPS) with local assessments (formative and summative) and state assessments. Teachers use the online GOFAR to create benchmark assessments aligned to the state standards.

Content area teachers across teams and/or grade levels review curriculum maps, discuss how students can make connections from subject to subject, and plan integrated units of study.

Teachers develop performance tasks that require all learners to demonstrate a depth of knowledge to include such cognitive processes as explanation, interpretation, application, analysis of perspectives, empathy, and self-knowledge.

To monitor the implementation of the curriculum, the leadership team organizes targeted awareness walks with standards in hand. These targeted walks may be conducted by system and school leadership or content area or grade level teams. The targeted walks can occur monthly or as often as needed to provide an in-depth analysis of the implementation of the curriculum.

In the Area of Data Analysis and Utilization:

Formative and summative assessment data are routinely disaggregated to adjust implementation of the curriculum and improve instruction.

Teachers regularly analyze student work according to the CC/GPS standards to determine if students are meeting or exceeding grade level expectations. Based on the analysis and use of current research, teachers make decisions to better meet student needs.

Student data from state assessment results is disaggregated to identify patterns for specific students or groups of students. Grade level and/or content area teachers and administrators collaborate to analyze data to determine learning priorities for the school improvement plan.

School leadership meets with individual teachers to review their grade level outcomes by content area and to discuss the teacher's plan for meeting individual student academic needs.

School leadership monitors the implementation of the teachers' action plans and provides support as needed. Monitoring may occur in many different ways to include a review of formative classroom data on a regular basis, periodic teacher-leadership conferences, and classroom observations.

Teachers provide students with specific commentary on student work and connect the comments to the elements within the standards. Teachers identify exemplary work that exemplifies the standard(s). Teachers refer to this work as a model of the expectations for performance. Teachers provide students with examples of work that meets standard(s) by creating a display that includes benchmark work, specific commentary as to how this work meets the standard, assessment criteria.

Once teachers have come to consensus on what students should know, understand, and be able to do, they collaboratively design assessments to gauge student progress throughout a unit of study (formative assessments) and to measure student achievement at the end of the unit of study (summative assessments). Once teachers administer the assessments they come together to analyze the results and revise instruction.

Teachers work collaboratively to create performance tasks and assessment criteria based on the standards and the elements of each standard. Teachers work through the tasks collaboratively to ensure validity and specificity to the element/standard.

Grade level and content area teachers administer diagnostic assessments at the beginning of each unit of study to design instruction to build on student strengths, to clarify misconceptions, and introduce new or unknown concepts.

Informal, formative assessments are embedded in teaching and learning activities, are explicitly aligned to the standards, and used to revise instruction.

Teachers use teaching and scoring rubrics as a guideline for assessing and evaluating student work and performance.

*Scoring rubrics: Scoring rubrics are guides that enable teachers to make reliable judgments about student work and enable students to self-assess their work.

*Teaching rubrics: Teaching rubrics, developed with students, define and describe quality work in language students can understand. They are used by students to assess their works in progress and thereby guide revision and improvement. Teaching rubrics are created as a result of the teaching that has taken place in the classroom, not prior to instruction.

Students are given opportunities to present their work orally to peers to receive specific feedback for improvement. Students provide feedback to each other in a variety of settings to include, peer response groups, cooperative groups, and/or during a closing meeting such as author's chair, reader's chair, or a math closing.

Teachers understand the different types and purposes of assessment and evaluation. This may include authentic, screening, formative, summative, informal, diagnostic, and/or performance assessments. Teachers use this knowledge to determine the most effective assessments to measure student progress.

In the Area of Instructional Best Practices:

Students maintain a record of their work in products such as, student folders and portfolios, for the purpose of noting progress in meeting the standards. Teachers utilize these records to adjust instruction to meet student needs.

Students not meeting standard(s) are grouped according to assessment results and are assigned to safety net instruction which occurs before, during, and after school.

Teachers and administration work together to research and select organizing frameworks that align standards, assessments, and instruction. The design of the curriculum maps, units, and lessons formats enable teachers to know what student should understand and be able to do.

The instructional design team or leadership team develops a rollout plan to implement the organizing framework and coordinate professional learning, support, and monitoring. This plan includes support structures such as modeling by coaches or lead teachers, model classrooms, peer observation schedules, study groups, and teacher meetings.

The school schedule is designed to reflect designated times for common content area teacher meetings, grade, or team meetings, and vertical planning meetings. Most learning team meetings are scheduled during common planning periods, and teachers meet during the school day each week.

Teachers meet to agree upon a common understanding of the standards and elements by reviewing the standards, elements, and benchmark student work (e.g. anchor papers, exemplars, projects). Teachers collect exemplary student work to clarify mastery of standards or specific elements. They analyze student work samples to plan and revise units or lessons, develop specific studies around common topics.

The media specialist collaborates with the instructional staff to determine media center support needed to increase resources to enhance school-wide content. A process is in place to communicate the reading levels of students to the media specialists. The media specialist serves on the leadership team and provides services and resources that support school units and lesson implementation.

The expected understanding of units and lessons are determined collaboratively by teachers and are based on the standards for the subject and/or grade level. Essential questions, enduring understandings, or lesson goals use the language of the standards/elements appropriate for the lesson. The teacher explains the learning goals and the vocabulary of the standard. The language of the standard is referenced throughout the lesson.

Time is scheduled to communicate summative and formative assessment results to students. Teachers work with students to establish learning goals based on their assessment results and the standards. Student conferences may be held with the teacher, administrators, graduation coach, peers, parents or a combination of these persons to define student learning goals. Learning goals are written by the students as age appropriate.

Teacher instruction includes the identified needs of students, and flexible grouping is used to enable students to reach mastery of the standards and learning goals. A manageable assessment system is in place for teachers and students to maintain records of student mastery of standards and personal goals.

Using diagnostic and formative assessments, teachers group their students in a variety of ways to include, whole group, small group, cooperative learning pairs or groups, individual, interest-based, skills-based, knowledge-based, etc. The groups are interchangeable as student achievement progresses.

Teachers effectively use technology to provide real world application, to enhance students' research skills, and to differentiate instruction to maximize student learning. The technology activities used promote differentiation and instruction aligned to individual student needs. The technology used by teachers and students promote content research and require the conceptual application of the standards.

Teachers have clearly defined curriculum plans and expectations for meeting the standards in each subject area. The plans and expectations are discussed with the students as a whole group, in teacher-student conferences, as well as parent conferences. As a result, students write clear, meaningful, and personal goals based on the standards and summative or formative assessment results. As they strive to meet their goals, students use feedback to analyze and revise their work.

In the Area of Professional Learning

Faculty and staff read and discuss articles/ books on classroom instructional strategies, best practices, and innovative programs. The articles and books are used for collaborative planning and discussion.

Teachers are provided professional learning on the use of diagnostic and formative assessments and learning styles to strengthen flexible grouping practices.

Teachers work collaboratively to develop a clear, comprehensive plan to integrate technology into the curriculum as a means to motivate and support students' conceptual understanding and independent application of the core curriculum.

Collaborative teacher meetings are held to review and or design performance tasks and assignments. Teachers work professionally and collaboratively to review the tasks and assignments and discuss their alignment with grade/subject level learning goals, standards and elements. The assignments and tasks reflect the rigor and language of the standards. The assignments and tasks require explanation, interpretation, and conceptual application.

Teachers participate in professional learning on differentiated instruction. Appropriate support and follow-up is planned quarterly by the leadership team and in collaborative teacher meetings. Follow-up support may include planning teacher meetings on management of formative assessment data to guide differentiated instruction, facilitating work groups, varying tasks, etc., scheduling demonstration lessons and teacher observations, videotaping classes for additional professional learning.

Corrective Action Plan Initiated by Georgia DOE in August 2011 for TMS

Corrective Action Option: *Option 6: Restructure the internal organizational structure within the school (Leadership) Team expanded and reorganized to promote shared leadership.*

GSS Strands	Actions, Strategies, and Interventions	Person(s) Responsible	Means of Evaluation	
			Artifacts	Evidence of Impact on Student Learning
Instruction	Increase the number of school-wide collaborative meetings in reading, language arts, mathematics, science and social studies by grade level and content.	Principal, Assist. Prins., Ed. Evaluator, Dept. Chairs	Schedule of Collaborative Mtgs/Agendas/ Minutes	Benchmark assessments CDAs State scores

Curriculum	Provide curriculum resources and Teacher Keys support to facilitate best practices in curriculum development.	Principal, Assist. Prins., Ed. Evaluator, Dept. Chairs	Resource books, manipulatives, CLASS Keys artifacts, Observations	Benchmark assessments CDAs State scores
Professional Learning	Utilize county curriculum specialists, consultants, and teacher leaders at Turner to train and support teachers in the use of research-based instruction.	Math and Reading Teachers, Dept. Chairs	Agendas and Minutes from meetings	Benchmark assessments CDAs State scores
Leadership	Structure leadership within the school to include greater representation and responsibility among all departments and all grade levels using CCRPI as the framework.	Principal, Assist. Prins., Dept. Chairs, Leadership Team	Leadership meeting rosters, minutes, and agendas	Benchmark Assessments CDAs State scores
Instruction	Provide students with disabilities and general ed. students additional math support through an instructional coach, iPass technology, and math pull-outs during connections	Math Coach, TMS special ed. & gen. ed. teachers	Attendance rosters for classes	Benchmark Assessments CDAs State scores

RTI Letter for Parents

Dear Parent/Guardian of _____,

In our continuing efforts to improve the academic performance of all students, Turner Middle School is implementing the RTI system. RTI, Response to Intervention, is a system designed to provide effective interventions to meet the needs of students using scientific, research based interventions. RTI focuses on improving the educational performance of students who are at risk of not meeting state standards on the Milestones or other district level assessments. RTI identifies student needs and provides a continuum of increasingly intensive programming based on specific individual needs. The student's progress is directly and frequently monitored.

TMS students were identified for RTI using CRCT scores from the previous school year, AIMSweb Assessments, and/or current classroom performance. Based on your child's scores and/or classroom performance he/she was identified as a student who could benefit from additional instruction and practice.

In an effort to improve your child's skills in the areas of:
1) _____
2) _____
3) _____
4) _____
5) _____

he/she will participate in a small group or individual intervention. This intervention will take place once a week for approximately 20-40 minutes per session. The intervention(s) will allow your child to work at his/her current ability level and gain skills that are necessary to be a more successful student. In order to accurately assess student progress, the intervention(s) will be in effect for a minimum of 4-10 weeks.

We are committed to helping all students succeed. If you have any questions regarding RTI, please call 770-XXX-XXXX or visit our website.

Respectfully,

Sample of Student Identification for RTI					
Last Name	Grd	SCI	SS	Lexile	NOTES
Adams	7	787	802	780	
Aguirre	7	777	774	905	SPED
Amerson	7	779	815	980	Removed from Science on 9/16/13
Amerson	7	791	804	1145	Removed from Science on 9/16/13
Amos	7	789	800	1005	
Anderson	7	779	783	930	
Arrendondo	7	821	815		Added Reading 9/4
Bendolph	7	794	788	980	
Body	7	794	777	825	
Bonilla	7	782	772	755	
Borden	7	779	802	875	
Brooks	7	798	815	825	Math Enrichment 1st 9 weeks
Brown	7	753	794	955	
Butler	7	798	855	980	Removed from Science on 9/16/13
Camara	7	798	830	1005	Removed from Science on 9/16/13
Cannon	7	777	794	930	Removed from Science on 9/16/13
Carter	7	779	796	755	Math Enrichment 1st 9 weeks
Clark	7	798	810	875	Math Enrichment 1st 9 weeks
Clarke	7	763	774	670	SST
Colin Mora	7	784	800	710	Math Enrichment 1st 9 weeks
Correa	7	798	796	1005	

A Teacher that Led RTI – Dr. Amy Gilbert

From: Amy Gilbert
Subject: continued special education supports

Good evening,

In just a few short weeks, it is evident that the science supports we have begun to provide our SWD in 4th period are improving many dispositions, confidence, and participation in class. As you know we have 10 students in this class who require very specific instructional modifications. After hearing and responding to my pleas for your support, there have been many effective changes that have positively impacted our students!

For example, in the first hour of instruction Mr. Beall is concentrating on 4-5 of these students through redirection and prompting. This is proving invaluable. It is exactly the kind of support that was needed so that my attention could be directed toward others.

Of further positive note, the vocabulary instruction (previewing) Ms. Grady is providing in the last 30 minutes is improving their vocabulary acquisition. These students are already doing a better job of using vocabulary in their written and oral explanations during the regular class time. At this same time Ms. Gray is now pulling 2-4 other students who need additional time to complete classwork tasks (accommodation), while the remaining 20+ students are left with me to complete a novel study (enrichment).

My point in all this.....As I met with Dr. Osindele today I honestly and openly elaborated on the changes we have begun to make. I shared with her both the way we have begun to collaborate to provide these students with quality instruction and the effective communication that is allowing these supports to be sustainable. As I expressed with you all a few months ago, meeting these students' needs requires all of us. Dr. Osindele agreed. She expressed that what we are trying to do is "innovative" and "differentiation at its best." I felt you all should know her commendations.

As we move forward in our semester, the current unit is coming to an end. Therefore, I have attached a new set of vocabulary cards to use in pre-teaching the upcoming terms, the student learning map for the unit, and a template for recording definitions/pictures. The sequencing of pre-teaching is outlined below.

- Categories of Waves
- Structure of Waves
- Characteristics of Electromagnetic Waves
- Characteristics of Mechanical Waves

I am also happy to meet with everyone again so that we can discuss the outcome of other resources that were provided in our last meeting, and determine how/if modifications and/or new resources are needed. Please let me know an available time for everyone.

Sample Data – Dr. Amy Gilbert

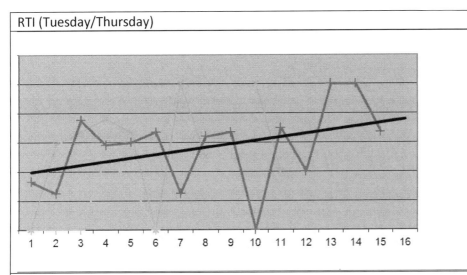

RTI (Tuesday/Thursday)

Goal/Interventions
Improve both reading comprehension and understandings of science/social studies concepts   Use of visuals to make sense of concepts within text
(same)   Use of evidence within the text to make sense of new/unknown concepts

Goal/Interventions
Increase ability to read, analyze, and interpret raw data; to apply meanings to the outcomes of specific scientific inquiries   Use science and social studies resources to investigate situations that supports student in conducting investigations as well as presenting/analyzing investigation results
Vocabulary acquisition and application   Use of memory cards, visuals, and graphic organizers specific to math and science
Solve expressions   Use of kinesthetic models and virtual demonstrations to solve expressions

Counselor Duties for RTI

RTI:

Assist grade level team in Identifying Tier II students
Send letters home to contact parents
(Teachers assist in contacting parents if letters aren't returned)
Monitor data entry for the team (remind teachers to consistently input data)
Assist in scheduling RTI remediation days
Attend grade level meetings to discuss RTI progress, new referrals, or dismissals

Teacher Reflection of RTI Effectiveness

From: Franklin
Sent: Wednesday, October 15, 2014 5:13 PM
To: Kwame Carr
Subject: Data Request

As I reflected on your request, I wanted to provide data, so you could determine whether it was useful to you or not. Despite that, I attempted to provide data that provides relevance to your work here as well as across the district. The attached data is a comparison of my student's performance on the CDA by item. Since I teach 6th grade, the school would be indicative of the scores the other 6th grade SS teacher would have scanned by 12:45. That teacher student's took their CDA today, so not all of their scores are in the system. Approximately 97% of my students are reflected in my scores.

How is data useful? Well, at least for the time and the standard/element to which it aligns, it gives me, you, the Department Chair, and the grade level administrator some insight into how my students compare. It also identifies what might I need to focus on over the next 9 week time frame to improve mastery. Correlations to those items could be made in order to focus my work and convey to students what our weaknesses are by standard. Eventually, this could lead to student conferences and student-led conferences with the parents and teachers. The student would lead the conference. Before that happens, we must have more consistent us of assessments as well as assessments that have sufficient items that give a true picture of each standard/element.

From our training today, I was living proof that teachers need more work on writing and formatting assessments. I have models, but I wanted to be authentic to the work you are doing here as well as where Turner is in its evolution of using consistent common assessment data to further target improvements in student's mastery of the content. My latest assessment data (Conflict and Change) can be paired with other results to begin developing differentiation and extension supports for my students. I am not that far yet though.

I hope that has been helpful and not just a waste of your time by reading and reviewing this information.

Requesting RTI Students during Planning

From: Purcell
Sent: Tuesday, October 21, 2014 4:17 PM
To: Turner Middle
Subject: 6th Math RTI -- Purcell and Kennedy

Please excuse the following students on **Wednesdays during 5th period** to attend Math RTI in Ms Kennedy's room. All students attending RTI have a blue laminated pass and have been instructed to check in with their connections teacher before reporting to RTI.

- **Acevedo**
- **Ambrose**
- **Beatty**
- **Bolton**
- **Carrillo**
- **Duradula**
- **Garcia**
- **Gutierrez**
- **Henson**
- **Hernandez**
- **Huerta**
- **Johnson-Martinez**
- **Martinez**
- **McClenton**
- **Nworgu**
- **Padron**

Principle 7 – Meetings

College & Career Ready Performance Index Faculty/Leadership Meetings (CCRPI)

3- MINUTE Maximum Presentation for each line item

1. Welcome and Opening Business
2. Gifted Report and Presentation
3. Language Arts/Writing Department <u>Data Report</u> & Presentation
4. Reading Department <u>Data Report</u> & Presentation
5. Math Department <u>Data Report</u> & Presentation
6. Science Department/Science Fair <u>Data Report</u> & Presentation
7. Social Studies <u>Data Report</u> & Presentation
8. Special Education <u>Data Report</u> & Presentation
9. Counselors Presentation
10. STEM Report & Presentation
11. Foreign Language Report & Presentation
12. Student Learning Objectives (SLO) Report & Presentation
13. 6th, 7th, 8th Grade Level Reports & Presentation
14. ESOL Report & Presentation
15. SLDS (...to replace FitnessGram)
16. Technology Report & Presentation
17. After School Programs Report & Presentation
18. PBIS Data
19. Administrative Report & Closing Business

* ALL Data Reports must include **school-wide** RTI data and all members of each department are expected to contribute to the overall process. <u>The data must reflect ***student engagement in the process*** and achievement based upon our measureable student achievement goals on the CCRPI.</u>

| Meeting Sign-In Sheet - Sample |

NAME   ROLE
(Please check appropriate box.)

	☐ Parent ☐ Teacher ☐ School Staff ☐ Administrator ☐ Community Member ☐ CO Staff ☐ Parent Outreach ☐ Other (please indicate) _____
	☐ Parent ☐ Teacher ☐ School Staff ☐ Administrator ☐ Community Member ☐ CO Staff ☐ Parent Outreach ☐ Other (please indicate) _____
	☐ Parent ☐ Teacher ☐ School Staff ☐ Administrator ☐ Community Member ☐ CO Staff ☐ Parent Outreach ☐ Other (please indicate) _____
	☐ Parent ☐ Teacher ☐ School Staff ☐ Administrator ☐ Community Member ☐ CO Staff ☐ Parent Outreach ☐ Other (please indicate) _____
	☐ Parent ☐ Teacher ☐ School Staff ☐ Administrator ☐ Community Member ☐ CO Staff ☐ Parent Outreach ☐ Other (please indicate) _____

| As You Lead Meetings, Realize… |

"And the survey says…what frustrates people most about meetings at work?"
[The top 10 responses were...]

1. Allowing attendees to ramble and repeat the same comments and thoughts.
2. Doesn't start on time, stay on track, or finish on time.
3. No specific action items or walk-away points.
4. No clear purpose or objective.
5. Not inspiring or motivating.
6. Not organized. No agenda.
7. Too long.
8. Repeating information for late arrivals.
9. Weak presenter (unprepared, monotone, overly redundant).
10. Boring. Nothing new or interesting.

Sample of Attendance Reporting

From: Alicia
Sent: Wednesday, October 15, 2014 11:59 PM
To: Kwame Carr
Subject: Attendance data from counselors

There are seventeen students in 6th grade with three or more unexcused absences. I have attempted to contact all seventeen parents. Three of the seventeen students have five or more absences. The students were reported to the school's social worker.

Only **4** kids in 7th grade with 5 or more unexcused absences.

8th grade 19 with 3 or more absences. 7 with 5 or more absences. Three were referred to Social worker.

Sample of 6th Grade Reporting

Sample of Math Reporting

6th Grade

We RTI all 6th math students at the same time.
We RTI 32 students this quarter.
We had 26 last quarter.
We have five additional students who are still in RTI but are in Ms Grier's class this quarter.
We are using IPass and focusing on remediation of fraction operations.
Our 29 October scores increased 37.8% from our baseline scores taken in August.

7th Grade

There are 38 students in RTI for 7th grade.
Aimsweb MCOMP is used for tracking.

7% are well below average.
36% are average
28% are above average
29% are well above average

8th Grade
Thus far because of scheduling conflicts and Science/Social Studies having priority overall, I have consistently been serving 6 students out of 15.
2/3 of this group have shown little to some growth, while 1/3 has shown a 25% gain in their probe scores.

I will be increasing my number of RTI sessions to include a Monday session during 6th period, and intensifying my methods for the students who are showing little or no growth by individualizing my instruction efforts.
SPED

48 students served
42% are near their target
42% are above their target
14% have insufficient data because they are new to our school
2% below their target

As a general rule: NO meetings are to be scheduled over ONE HOUR – that goes for parent meetings, faculty meetings, teacher meetings, concerts, awards programs, continuation ceremony…EVERYTHING!!! – Stay on Task

Principle 8 – Professional Learning

Professional Learning Strategies

How to Facilitate Adult Learning Environments

Professional Development Strategies:	*Explanation*
Study Groups	books, topics, procedures, teachers, etc.
Action Research	teachers studying their own best practices
Observations/Modeling	teachers learning from one another
Find someone different…	share ideas, experiences, beliefs
Talk in your group about…	compare thoughts and ideas about a topic
Come up front…	to view an overhead or presentation (movement)
Get in a circle…	share one thing you've learned
Read and share…	assign sections, summarize, and share
Analyze the data…	provide data and allow to reflect on implications
Create a lesson…	create performance tasks, lesson plans, etc.
Solve a problem…	assign real life examples for teachers to solve
Popcorn responses…	allow people to reflect aloud randomly
Reflect and share…	assign a quote, allow reflection, share thoughts
Does anyone have…	a story, an experience, or an idea of relevance
Accessing Student Voices…	see **Powerful Designs** book for remaining topics
Assessment as Professional Development	"
Case Discussion	"
Classroom Walk-Throughs	"
Critical Friends Groups	"
Curriculum Designers	"

Immersing Teachers in Practice	"
Journaling	"
Lesson Study	"
Mentoring	"
Peer Coaching	"
Portfolios for Educators	"
School Coaching	"
Shadowing Students	"
Standards in Practice	"
Training the Trainer	"
Tuning Protocols	"
Visual Dialogue	"

<u>*Characteristics of Positive Adult Learning Experiences*</u>:

Hands-on & Interactive

Relevant Topic

Ready-to-use (Immediate Ideas and Materials)

Speaker relates to audience/shares relevant experiences

Organized presentation with appropriate "Flow" (always better to go fast than slow)

Good Humor

Good Hooks & Closures

Suitable Environment (Food, Temp, Not too Crowded)

Adhere to Timeframes

Always give LESS time than is needed with uneven times for task completion

5 Ways to Model Mathematics = Real World Problems, Manipulatives, Oral Language, Written Symbols, Pictures

How to Organize Training Blocks for Adult Learners (70 – 90 minutes)

Hook	=	**10 min**
Direct Instruction	=	**20 min**
Group Work	=	**30 – 40 min**
Sharing	=	**10 min**
Processing/Reflection	=	**10 min**

Critical Notes for Educators…to Share with Staff:	*Reference Principle # 3*

Hope Conference Notes (2007 – Marietta, GA):	*Reference Principle # 3*

Feedback to a Principal is Also Professional Learning

From: Mary
Sent: Wednesday, May 14, 2014 9:41 AM
To: Kwame Carr
Subject: Feedback

Good Morning,

I hope your day goes well! My visit to Turner MS on yesterday confirms all of the positive things I have heard from my team members. You are providing the leadership that is moving your teachers and students toward higher student achievement. It was a wonderful end to my day to see a group of teachers who are embracing what data-driven instruction and school improvement really means. The actions that you all have taken are to be commended. I especially like the following:

1. The emphasis placed on identification and individual support of students in the RTI process. Teachers not only knew the students but provided aligned interventions, the tool used to monitor those interventions and
    their movement out of the process or improvement made during the process.
2. All facets of your school are reviewed including performing arts, P.E., technology, PBIS, etc.
3. The monitoring of the tutorial program is to be commended.
4. Monitoring the progress of SWD.
5. Monitoring of your mentoring program.
6. Celebrations for meeting expectations.
7. SWD interviewed after testing to gather information for adjustments next school year.

The following are suggestions for extending what is already being done (just suggestions and all will not be possible in one year):
1. Similar to your STEM day, hold a technology week where student are exposed to business and industry leaders' use of technology and then design a project across content areas.
2. Expand your AR program to including book checkout for summer with a student and parent awards day at end of summer for those who meet previously determined criteria.
3. This may be happening, honor a parent volunteer with a monthly award for involvement and/or participation.
4. Award students or groups of students for building or maintaining positive school culture.
5. Extend your STEM technology piece to include more one-to-one devices (maybe start with an 8th grade content area) to include students manning the help desk. This could be an afterschool technology club.

6. Extend the school culture practices to include a wellness program.
7. For your presentation at MRESA: It will be powerful if there was a video so others could see your CCRPI Faculty Meetings. Include data presented on chart paper (one of your presenters did this), the interventions, next steps that I saw yesterday and add current CRCT data.

Finally as discussed, do not forget about professional learning for you and your assistant principals. I attached the Turnaround Principles and a sample rubric to guide you toward meeting your personal growth goals. Keep these in mind when planning your next professional learning steps. You are on your way to becoming a Turnaround Principal!

It is a pleasure to serve Turner MS,
Mary

Defining Professional Learning at Your School

From: Kwame Carr
Sent: Wednesday, November 16, 2011 3:48 PM
Subject: Professional Learning (TMS)

Professional Learning at Turner 2011 – 2012

- ✓ Turner Instructional Design implementation – ongoing – **attached below**
- ✓ Learning Focused Schools – ongoing redelivery – beginning stages of implementation
- ✓ RTI – each grade level
- ✓ System 44 – special education implementation
- ✓ Teacher Keys – ongoing
- ✓ Content Department Meetings – each grade level - based on identified weaknesses
- ✓ ThinkGate data analysis
- ✓ Student Longitudinal Data System analysis
- ✓ AimsWEB analysis

CCRPI Faculty Meetings led by Departments starting Nov. 8, 2011

Book studies - To Be Added in January 2012

Instructional Design IS Professional Learning

PRE-TEACHING (Before the lesson…collaboration is required with artifacts as evidence)

1. <u>Collaboratively</u> identify the Power Standards - **Use CDAs**
2. <u>Collaboratively</u> create curriculum maps with standard pacing and an off/pace modified map
3. <u>Individually/Collaboratively</u> study and know your content, vocabulary and skills presented by the standards and elements by:
   a. Individually and collaboratively reading through the standards and associated elements
   b. Making appropriate connections, thinking about possible combinations
   c. Reading through the appropriate sections in the textbook
   d. Reviewing other textbooks and resources
   e. Reviewing the content descriptors (if available) for the standards and elements taught
   f. Identifying and weaving vocabulary into the lesson, referring to them often in context
   g. Recognizing the importance of acquiring vocabulary as it relates to student learning of standards
4. <u>Collaboratively</u> match the levels of cognition with the standard/element
5. <u>Collaboratively</u> organize to teach in ascending order OR order of cognitive rigor and relevance; discuss and recommend a progressive level of questioning
6. <u>Collaboratively</u> create essential and daily focus questions
7. <u>Collaboratively</u> create summative assessments
8. <u>Collaboratively</u> create formative assessments
9. <u>Collaboratively</u> select appropriate instructional strategies – not too many
10. <u>Collaboratively</u> place plan into the required planning format; provide to classroom guests
11. <u>Collaboratively</u> prepare or select lesson documents/artifacts including rubrics; provide to guests

TEACHING (During the lesson…peer observations, modeling, coaching, videotaping, etc.)

12. Teach Your Students by:
    a. Conspicuously posting standards/elements on board or wall and present to students; connect to prior standard or current EQ (essential question)
    b. Conspicuously posting and stating EQ
    c. Unwrapping the standard
    d. Conspicuously posting and stating the FQ (focus question)
    e. Presenting vocabulary in context during the lesson
    f. Opening and teaching the acquisition lesson using cognitively appropriate best practice strategy
    g. Teaching using cognitively appropriate questions
    h. Scaffolding students and fully developing the lesson and concepts being presented to the level of rigor required by the verb in the standard
    i. Making relevant real-world connections

j. Conducting mini-summary checks, every 15 minutes (led by teacher(s) and/or students)
  k. Closing the lesson
  l. Formatively assessing students at the cognitive level taught and use the data to re-teach
  m. Re-teaching and/or reinforcing, if necessary
  n. Summatively assessing students to determine mastery
  o. If no mastery, then re-teach; If mastery, then move on (mastery must be at 80%)

POST-TEACHING **(After the lesson…collaboration is required with artifacts as evidence)**

13. <u>Collaboratively</u> plan to give feedback after the common summative assessment (within 2 – 3 days)
14. <u>Collaboratively</u> decide best use of data to re-teach using a different strategy at the same cognitive level required (may involve extra and personal time)
15. <u>Communicate</u> summative results within 2 to 3 days of the assessment; move on if the mastery number for your subject meets or exceeds expectations. Weigh the need to master vs. the need to move on based on the curriculum map (This requires your professional judgment)

Notes on the Original Karate Kid Movie – Best Professional Learning for Teachers

What Teachers can Learn from The Karate Kid (1984)

- Teacher made the decision to teach the student (i.e. was not forced)
- Karate from a book? – That's Nonesense!!!!!
- Do something unexpected to show you care (the bike scene)
- Trust the picture inside of you (trees)
- When students are in trouble, save the day (shower scene)
- The problem is the attitude (boys)
- No such thing as a bad student, only bad teachers
- Teacher say, student do
- Stand and don't flinch, you're the expert (the confrontation)
- Winning or losing doesn't matter, it's about earning respect
- Don't walk the middle of the road (do it or don't do it, otherwise get broken in two)
- Use real-life experiences to teach (sanding, washing, waxing, etc.)
- Be the teacher, the genius, the unexplained, the mystic, in students' eyes
- "Man that catches a fly with chopsticks can accomplish anything"
- High repetition and practice (paint the fence, paint the house, sand the deck, wax the cars)
- Student felt like a slave, didn't understand
- Student wanted to quit, tried to quit
- Demand excellence, explain when it's time to explain
- Spend enormous amounts of time on basics, which leads to awesome combinations and foresights (knowing what to do)
- It's okay to be unorthodox

- Have a plan already in mind and work your plan to your advantage (fishing)
- You don't take karate to learn to fight, you take karate so you don't have to fight
- You don't teach to save people, you teach so you don't have to save people
- The teacher was never tired, the teacher had fun
- The teacher incorporated their own culture into education
- The teacher had their own issues (letdowns in life)
- At times, the student took care of the teacher
- A relationship existed, and it was personal
- Student wanted to be like the teacher, started practicing all alone, was inspired
- Teacher began sharing secrets, shortcuts (how to strike)
- Instruction must be quality over quantity
- Teacher didn't think for the student, taught student to think for themselves (it mattered what student thought of themselves)
- Everything must have balance (life)
- License doesn't replace eyes, ears, and brain (driving)
- Teacher's life experience was different, yet he prepared student for times he never experienced
- Survived even when the enemy tried to put him out of commission

Insights by Kwame A. Carr

Assessment Writing, Technology Integration, Cultural Awareness = BIG 3

Train your teachers in the aforementioned BIG 3 to get results!!!!!!!!!

Principle 9 – Instructional and Curricular Protocols and Design

Backwards Design Defined as Professional Learning/Collaboration & Instructional Design: You KEEP seeing this because everything boils down to THIS!!!!!!!!!!!!!!

PRE-TEACHING (Before the lesson...collaboration is required with artifacts as evidence)

1. <u>Collaboratively</u> identify the Power Standards - **Use CDAs**
2. <u>Collaboratively</u> create curriculum maps with standard pacing and an off/pace modified map
3. <u>Individually/Collaboratively</u> study and know your content, vocabulary and skills presented by the standards and elements by:
    a. <u>Individually and collaboratively</u> reading through the standards and associated elements
    b. Making appropriate connections, thinking about possible combinations
    c. Reading through the appropriate sections in the textbook
    d. Reviewing other textbooks and resources
    e. Reviewing the content descriptors (if available) for the standards and elements taught
    f. Identifying and weaving vocabulary into the lesson, referring to them often in context
    g. Recognizing the importance of acquiring vocabulary as it relates to student learning of standards
4. <u>Collaboratively</u> match the levels of cognition with the standard/element
5. <u>Collaboratively</u> organize to teach in ascending order OR order of cognitive rigor and relevance; discuss and recommend a progressive level of questioning
6. <u>Collaboratively</u> create essential and daily focus questions
7. <u>Collaboratively</u> create summative assessments
8. <u>Collaboratively</u> create formative assessments
9. <u>Collaboratively</u> select appropriate instructional strategies – not too many
10. <u>Collaboratively</u> place plan into the required planning format; provide to classroom guests
11. <u>Collaboratively</u> prepare or select lesson documents/artifacts including rubrics; provide to guests

TEACHING (During the lesson...peer observations, modeling, coaching, videotaping, etc.)

12. Teach Your Students by:
    a. Conspicuously posting standards/elements on board or wall and present to students; connect to prior standard or current EQ (essential question)
    b. Conspicuously posting and stating EQ
    c. Unwrapping the standard
    d. Conspicuously posting and stating the FQ (focus question)
    e. Presenting vocabulary in context during the lesson
    f. Opening and teaching the acquisition lesson using cognitively appropriate best practice strategy
    g. Teaching using cognitively appropriate questions

    h. Scaffolding students and fully developing the lesson and concepts being presented to the level of rigor required by the verb in the standard
    i. Making relevant real-world connections
    j. Conducting mini-summary checks, every 15 minutes (led by teacher(s) and/or students)
    k. Closing the lesson
    l. Formatively assessing students at the cognitive level taught and use the data to re-teach
    m. Re-teaching and/or reinforcing, if necessary
    n. Summatively assessing students to determine mastery
    o. If no mastery, then re-teach; If mastery, then move on (mastery must be at 80%)

POST-TEACHING **(After the lesson…collaboration is required with artifacts as evidence)**

13. <u>Collaboratively</u> plan to give feedback after the common summative assessment (within 2 – 3 days)
14. <u>Collaboratively</u> decide best use of data to re-teach using a different strategy at the same cognitive level required (may involve extra and personal time)
15. <u>Communicate</u> summative results within 2 to 3 days of the assessment; move on if the mastery number for your subject meets or exceeds expectations. Weigh the need to master vs. the need to move on based on the curriculum map (This requires your professional judgment)

Instructional Framework…adopt a framework such as:

Learning Focused Schools (LFS).

Your school needs ONE framework and EVERYONE needs to work it!!!!!!!!

CDA Protocols (Protocols for <u>Common District Assessments</u> given District-wide)

CDA NON-NEGOTIABLES/EXPECTATIONS

NOTE: TMS Instructional Design Plan IS Backward Design

Backward design – it is okay to review assessments prior to planning for and teaching a unit.
Assessments must be administered as directed within the set window of time.
CDAs are the unit tests.
The CDA grade goes into Thinkgate and the grade book.
Teacher made tests can be given following re-teaching.
If a retest is given, the CDA grade and the retest grade go into the grade book.
The CDA grade is not to be replaced or averaged.
CDAs cannot be altered.
CDAs will remain in place when Milestones assessments are implemented.
CDA scores should be counted as a regular test.
No CDA score can be dropped from a child's grade.
The only modifications that can be made to a CDA is for students with an IEP/504 plan.
Teachers must give all CDAs that have been created.
After the CDAs, any remaining unit assessments should be created in school-based PLCs.
No CDAs should be taken home with students.
Teachers must abide by the teacher directions provided for each assessment.

Raising the Bar on Special Education : 6-Step Process

From: Kwame Carr
Sent: Tuesday, September 3, 2013 3:24 PM
Subject: Raising the Bar on Special Ed (6-Step Process)

Greetings TMS Special Education Teachers,

As you know, I'll be evaluating the special education department this year, perhaps for the next several years. We have been designated a Focus School in the state of Georgia, which means, <u>by definition</u>:

85% of all other special education departments/special education students in Title 1 Schools in Georgia perform better than ours in one or more measurements.

I don't believe that, and I never will. The only other school with a designation in our county is Inner Harbor, which is a residential Priority School. Our Focus designation is totally unacceptable given our student population. I've worked in several schools K-12 across two districts, and I can tell you with absolute confidence that our students and our school have no business on the Focus Schools list. With that said, these are the immediate changes I'm expecting:

1. *Collaborative input of grades* among co-teachers - there is no longer a "these are my students" attitude - each teacher, after reaching a consensus, has the right to enter student grades
2. *Collaborative input in the "accommodation" process* - altering a grade is NOT an accommodation
3. *Collaborative effort in ensuring high expectations for all students* - what we've been doing is not working. That's why 85% of schools do better
4. *Collaborative communication with parents/guardians* - any teacher has the right to call a student's parent at TMS, whether they teach that child or not, but especially if they do
5. *Use of the SWD performance targets set by the state* to set your personal SWD goal/target for 2014.
6. *Pulling SWD students in their areas of weakness* during our school-wide "RTI" process for reading, language arts, math, science, social studies during planning time

I realize some teachers wanted to express some "concerns" regarding special education. Frankly, my concern is being a Focus School, the only one in Douglas County. I will continue to listen very intently to any real concerns, with the understanding that anything resembling low expectations and/or excuses for low achievement on a teacher's behalf will dismiss that concern. Saying that, "Mr. Carr doesn't understand special education" is one such excuse that will be readily dismissed. Attempting to alter or explain away the aforementioned expectations in #1 - #6 will also be readily dismissed.

Please be prepared to meet with me individually on Friday, September 6th, 2013, to discuss your personal game plan for improvement and to reach our student achievement goals.

| **Instructional Protocols - Faculty Meeting Agenda** |

1) Assessment Writing Follow-Up / Using Curriculum Maps / Frameworks / Moodle
   - **Assistant Principals Fredenburg and Rowe - 20 minute**s
2) ThinkGate Enhancement
   - **Mr. Franklin - 20 minutes**
3) TMS – Instructional Protocols & Policies
   - **Mr. Carr - 30 minutes**

   I. Grading Policy – 50% Summative requires <u>**MINIMUM of 6 summatives per semester**</u>
   II. Collaborative Planning Is What You Asked For… (Use Backwards Design)
   III. Leadership – Standing for Something Relentlessly – No Faking
   IV. Work Ethic of a Leader is Continuous – Pace Yourself for the Year – 365 days not 180
   V. Redefining What We Do As Georgia Adopts Milestones Assessment (Rigor)

Academic Content Department Chair Responsibilities & Expectations

The Department Chairperson serves as the primary instructional leader in the department and fulfills both teaching and leadership duties and responsibilities. The Department Chairperson is key in providing leadership and preserving the instructional integrity of the department. The Department Chairperson provides <u>**leadership in the areas of instructional improvement**</u>, and curriculum development. The Department Chairperson provides educational guidance, support, and leadership to the staff to ensure the district's educational goals are being met and to promote student success.

<u>The responsibility for the quality of instruction and the level of student success rests primarily on the classroom teacher</u>, but the Chairperson and other leadership positions have the responsibility to assist the classroom teacher in achieving success. The Instructional Lead Teacher (ILT) supervises and guides the department chairs and is held accountable by the principal to assist each content chair.

Responsibilities:

Under the general supervision of the site Principal and Instructional Lead Teacher, and in coordination with the Assistant Superintendent of Instruction and Leadership, the *Department Chairperson* will be responsible for the following:

1. Serve as an instructional leader to promote effective teaching strategies to ensure student mastery of State Standards **using backward design AND Learning Focused Framework**

2. Serve as a resource for department members

3. Work with the department members to understand and establish specific goals

4. **Willingness to promote new researched based strategies and best practices**

5. Implement relevant strategies being used to increase student achievement, specifically RTI

6. Work with the *School Improvement Specialist and Instructional Lead Teacher* for that subject area to monitor data team and collaborative meetings

7. Work with assigned department(s) to share best practices in an organized friendly format

8. Serve as a leader and support in the department including:

- Support a positive learning environment
- Assist in assessing professional development needs of members of the department
- Promote high expectations with all members of the department

9. Represent department positions and concerns at both the school and district level by:

- Convening timely meetings with the department to provide information from district level meetings
- Representing the department at District Curriculum Meetings as well as any other meetings specified by the site principal (If you are unable to attend the meeting, send a representative in your place and notify your site principal and School Improvement Specialist)
- Identifying and recommending possible solutions to school/department problems

10. Assist in the selection, ordering and distribution of textbooks, equipment and instructional materials and supplies as appropriate to the department and the School Plan

11. Any other duties or responsibilities assigned by the site principal.

Learning Focused : Increase Teacher Effectiveness and Accelerate Learning

Acceleration includes these *proactive supports*:

- Previewing (e.g. advance organizers – EQs, Vocabulary, Websites, Readings)
- Vocabulary Instruction
- Double Dosing
- Scaffolding
- Differentiated Assignments
- Remediation
- Review

Step 1: Previewing for Struggling Students (individually or small group)

Step 2: Previewing for All Students (whole group)

Step 3: Grade Level Instruction for All Students (whole group and/or flex group) with Scaffolding and Differentiation Strategies for identified Students – Ex: ESOL : SWD Students Perform Best When Given Regular Instruction (nationwide)

Step 4: Remediation (small group or individually) = RTI @ TMS

Formative High Impact Practices (F.I.P. = Formative Instructional Practices)

1. Use Descriptive Feedback to Help Students Improve – Similar to our Writing Process
2. Have Students Communicate Regularly Where they are in Their Learning
3. Have Students use Self-Assessment and Peer Feedback

*Note: Formative Assessment also involves STUDENTS and their ability to communicate learning with peers and to self-assess. Formative Assessment has been traditionally seen as a teacher's tool, but the High Impact Practices involve students in their learning.

Chunk and Check…

Every 12 to 15 minutes DURING the lesson, formatively

DOE: Identify the D.O.K. – Depth of Knowledge

Activity and Discussion

What is (effective) Curriculum?

1. Standards
2. Essential Questions
3. Vocabulary
4. Differentiation
5. Resources
6. Assessments

What is Explicit Instruction?

1) Setting the stage for learning (activities)
2) Clear expectations of what to do – stated clearly, in depth, leaving no room for error
3) Modeling the process
4) Guided Practice with corrective feedback
5) Independent Practice with constant feedback, checking for learning
6) Assessment that is relevant and meaningful to intended learning targets/standards
7) Closure/Summarizing

Maximizing Instructional Time

Maximizing instructional time requires forethought, organization, and implementation of a systemic plan for all teachers. Teachers must use comprehensive literacy strategies that are high impact-rapid response strategies, such as: previewing vocabulary, emphasizing reading comprehension, and writing across the curriculum to raise achievement. These strategies have been proven to boost student achievement, thereby, maximizing instructional time.

Another way to maximize instructional time is to provide students with learning maps prior to the delivery of instruction to prepare them for the next unit by allowing them to preview lessons. Vocabulary, essential questions, focus questions, key concepts, etc. must be addressed in learning maps. Learning maps need to be in the format of an advanced organizer and consistent among all teachers. Learning maps are especially effective for students performing below grade level.

It is important for instruction to be mapped at the beginning of the school year until the state mandated high-stakes test is administered. Common assessments must be developed that keep students on target, and instruction must be at the level of rigor required by the standards. Struggling students not meeting standards must be provided opportunities to accelerate during the school day. This can be accomplished using flexible scheduling or a school-wide uninterrupted instructional block of time.

Although reading and math are the foundations of education, we must remember that we are building future historians, artists, and scientists. We must differentiate instruction according to the interests of students and provide feedback, minute to minute, and use summarizing strategies. The formula for providing summarization, in minutes, is – the age of the student plus one. For example, a fourteen year old child needs a lesson summarized every fifteen minutes. Additionally, students must be responsible for summarizing, not teachers.

Maximizing instructional time requires many components. Educators must be aware of the purpose of their instruction and the use of best practices for gaining the highest achievement given the allotted time. Some tools to accomplish this goal include: learning maps, previewing vocabulary, writing, reading, advanced organizers, summarizing strategies, creative scheduling and acceleration strategies.

CITATION

Dutton, G (2011, April). *Exemplary practice from high poverty - high performing schools*. Paper presented at the April 9th meeting of School Assessment and Evaluation at Lincoln Memorial University, Cleveland, Tennessee.

Selecting Strategies on Rigor

- Brainstorming
- Community service
- Compare and contrast •Cooperative learning
- Creative arts
- Demonstration
- Games
- Group discussion
- Guided practice
- Inquiry
- Instructional technology
- Internship
- Lecture
- Literature
- Memorization
- Note-taking/graphic organizers
- Presentations/exhibitions
- Problem-based learning
- Project design
- Recognition and rewards
- Research & Writing
- Review and re-teaching
- Setting objectives and advanced organizers
- Simulation/role playing
- Socratic seminar
- Teacher questions
- Total physical response
- Video
- Work-based learning

Curriculum Strategies

1. Instructional Portfolio Review/Accountability Binder
2. Data Talks (School-wide – quarterly/annually)
3. SAMS/Checkpoints/Interims/Benchmarks
4. Common Assessments/Planning by subject or course teams
5. Lesson Plans (formative/summative data based upon AYP/SIP targets/goals)
6. Observations with other team members/observation critique with teacher
7. Academic Council formation (chairs, contacts, content)
8. Writing across curriculum (UGA, anchor papers, assigned times)
9. Reading across curriculum (selected readings, ITBS questions)
10. Remediation during the day/creative scheduling/ pullouts/support
11. Extended Days
12. Instructional coaches/model lessons/assist students
13. Data Support Specialist
14. Cognitive alignment/Lesson plans/Bloom's/Level of Cognition according to verbs in the standard
15. Mini-lessons based upon weaknesses
16. Professional learning communities by teams, weekly
17. Sub binders with specifications
18. GAPSS analysis of teachers
19. Standard Based Classrooms
20. Instructional Calendars based upon power standards
21. Workshops for the bubble students (winter and spring)
22. Competitions
23. Math/Science/Technology Night
24. Clubs
25. School-wide Mock Testing
26. 50% summative assessments/OAS/Achievement Series
27. Best Practices
28. Instructional Strategies

Principle 10 – Discipline

How to A.C.T. – A=admin, C=counselor, T=teacher	See Principle #2

Behavior	Who will handle behavior
1. Drugs, Alcohol, Tobacco, Weapons	A
2. Forgery/Cheating	T
3. Inappropriate School Behavior	T
4. Fighting	A
5. Theft	A
6. Being in a unauthorized area	T
7. Public display of affection	T
8. Vandalism	A
9. Sex Offenses, gestures, actions, etc.	A
10. Dress code violation	T
11. Profanity between students	T
12. Profanity towards an adult	T then A
13. Arson	A
14. Insubordination	T
15. Horseplay	T
16. Cutting class	T then A
17. Tardiness	T
18. Leaving class/campus	T then A
19. Breaking and entering	A
20. Cafeteria misbehavior	T
21. Open food or beverage, gum, etc.	T
22. Gambling	T
23. Minor disruptions in general	T
24. Inappropriate bus behavior	A
25. Chronic discipline problems	T then A
26. Repeated level III offenses (minor)	T
27. Nuisance item possession (phones)	T
28. Class disruptions	T
29. Failure to serve or complete ISS	A
30. Gang related activity/material	A
31. Threats/Bullying/Talk of Suicide	C
32. Suspected Child Abuse	A, C, T

Discipline Process…Teachers MUST Call Home before Writing a Referral, Barring an Emergency (fighting, physical or sexual assault, cursing the teacher out, etc.)

Discipline Infraction Referral Process

Flagrant Infractions	Routine Infractions
Provoking a fight	Disruptive Behavior
Forgery/Altercation of School Form	Failure to Serve Teacher Detention
Assault, Battery, Fighting	Gambling
Skipping Class, Leaving Campus Without Permission	Unexcused Tardies
Inappropriate Language Toward a Staff Member	Inappropriate Languages/Gestures

Flagrant Infractions	Routine Infractions
Smoking, Possession of Tobacco	False Information
Theft, Attempted Theft, Possession of Stolen Property(excludes cells, I-pods, electronic devices)	Cheating
Vandalism of School Property	Writing on a Desk
Possession of Weapons and or Drugs	Public Display of Affection

*All flagrant infractions must result in an immediate referral to the principal, assistant principal, assistant administrator or school resource officer.

I. Routine infractions must follow the three step referral process as outlined below each time an infraction occurs:

Step	Action Taken by the Teacher
1	Warn the student and **call the parent**
2	If the misbehavior continues, assign teacher detention and **contact the parent** to discuss the problem.

| 3 | If the misbehavior continues, **call the parent** and refer the student to the discipline administrator. |

II. Routine infractions for **Special Education** students must follow this five step referral process as outlined below **each** time the infraction occurs:

Step	Action Taken by the Teacher
1	Warn the student, visit the students BIP and **call the parent**.
2	If the misbehavior continues, meet with the student's Case Manager and follow the course of action on the BIP, **call the parent**.
3	If the misbehavior continues the Case Manager calls a Behavior Intervention Meeting with the IEP Committee, **advises the parent** that the next step will be a referral to the discipline office.
4	If the misbehavior continues, **call the parent** and refer the student to the discipline administrator.
5	Student's Case Manager, Teacher and Administrator meet to discuss the student's behavior.

PBIS (Positive Behavior Interventions and Supports) – Douglas County Schools, GA

In 2010, a group of school administrators, counselors, social workers, psychologists, community-service providers, parents, and students in the Douglas County community formed an advisory team to identify barriers to education in the district. They wanted to decrease barriers to mental health services, increase student attendance, increase student academic achievement, improve partnerships with community-based mental health providers and families through engagement and education, and create an environment where students feel safe to learn. This advisory team formed a new program called ADVOCATE SUCCESS: **Achieving Douglas' Vision of Counseling Approaches Toward Educational Success.**

The goal of the ADVOCATE SUCCESS team is to stand committed to the total development of character of all students, assess and promote the success of all students, and collaborate and support staff, students, parents, and the community in a shared vision of creating lifelong learners that are well-trained, passionate, and enthusiastic. The ADVOCATE SUCCESS team will carry out this goal by expanding the number of mental health professionals in each school, implementing a system of positive behavior interventions and supports in each school, and maintaining the Teachers As Advisors program in each school.

What is SW-PBIS?
School-wide Positive Behavior Interventions and Supports (SW-PBIS) or PBIS is a proactive systems approach for establishing the behavioral supports and social culture needed for all students in a school to achieve social, emotional, and academic success. PBIS applies a three-tiered system of support and a problem-solving process to enhance the capacity of schools to effectively educate all students

Positive Behavior Interventions and Supports emphasize:
- Optimizing academic instruction
- Teaching expected behaviors
- Modeling and practicing expected behaviors
- Reinforcing expected behaviors
- Pre-correcting to ensure expected behaviors are displayed

Why Are We Implementing SW-PBIS?
Previously, school-wide discipline has focused mainly on reacting to specific student misbehavior by implementing punishment-based strategies including reprimands, loss of privileges, office referrals, suspensions, and expulsions. Research has shown that the implementation of punishment, especially when it is used inconsistently and in the absence of other positive strategies, is ineffective. Introducing, modeling, and reinforcing positive social behavior is an important aspect of a student's educational experience. Teaching behavioral expectations and recognizing students for following them is a much more positive approach than waiting for misbehavior to occur before responding. The purpose of school-wide PBS is to establish a climate in which appropriate behavior is the norm.

The main goal of SW-PBIS is to create a positive school culture.
SW-PBIS makes the school environment predictable
- Everyone is speaking one common language
- Everyone shares a common vision (understanding of expectations)

School environment is positive
- Students receive regular recognition for positive behavior

School environment is safe
- There is a clear understanding that violent and disruptive behavior will not be tolerated and positive behavior is taught and not assumed

School environment is consistent
- All adults use similar expectations

Lesson Plans
Lesson plans are extremely important in the school wide positive behavior support process. It is the vehicle that is used to assure that students are actually taught what the expectations and behaviors that will be rewarded look like and sound like in various settings throughout the school. Without standardized lesson plans designed to be delivered

to all students, in all applicable settings, it is unrealistic to think that all students will know what is expected of them and be able to perform to the desired standard.

What is a PRIDE Ticket?

The PRIDE Ticket is a part of the incentive program for students at Turner Middle School. Students will earn signatures on their PRIDE Ticket for following the Student Code of Conduct which reinforces the 3 R's: **Respectful, Responsible, and Ready.**

How do students earn signatures on their PRIDE Ticket?

School-wide staff will recognize students who show PRIDE throughout the school day. Teachers are encouraged to give verbal positive reinforcement to students who demonstrate expected behaviors in addition to signing student PRIDE Tickets. How and when signatures are obtained on PRIDE Tickets are up to teacher/staff discretion. Teachers will sign a minimum of 5 PRIDE Tickets a day to his/her class and students they encounter through the school day.

Examples of behaviors that would merit PRIDE Ticket signatures:
- "Alex picked up another student's pencil and handed it back without being asked."
- "Keisha is following a procedure in the hallway while others are struggling."
- "Jason holds the door open for a student/teacher."
- "Miguel completed his classwork, homework, followed directions, or displayed some random act of kindness."

Why are we doing this?

We are doing this to teach students school procedures and expected behaviors in ALL settings giving us consistency while reinforcing positive behaviors and decreasing school-wide referrals.

What do students get for earning signatures on PRIDE Tickets?

Students will receive a variety of leveled prizes both tangible and non-tangible. Pride tickets will also earn student entry into PBIS celebrations.

Recognizing Success

- Students may have a chance to redeem PRIDE Tickets for weekly prizes
- A "Student of the Month" will receive school-wide recognition
- A "Faculty PRIDE Award" will be awarded monthly to an outstanding teacher/staff
- PRIDE Traits-Students who exhibit the monthly PRIDE Trait will receive school-wide recognition

STUDENT OF THE MONTH

A student who has demonstrated Turner Middle School PRIDE will be awarded with "Student of the Month"

- The student will be announced during morning/afternoon announcements
- The student's picture will be posted on the PBIS Bulletin Board
- Student will earn VIP access to PBIS celebration

- The student will receive an award

FACULTY PRIDE AWARD

(Determined by administration)
Each month a faculty member with one or all of the following criteria will receive an award:
1) An outstanding lesson plan that rigorously engages and challenges students
2) An outstanding lesson plan that fosters the ideas of respect towards others
2) Actively promotes the ideas of Turner Middle School PBIS daily in their classroom
- The faculty member will be announced during morning/afternoon announcements
- The faculty member's picture will be posted on the PBIS Bulletin Board
- The faculty member will receive an award

PRIDE TRAITS

(Determined by grade level staff)
Each month Turner Middle School will have a character trait. Examples of character traits include generosity, loyalty, honesty, and etc.
- The student will be announced during morning/afternoon announcements
- The student's picture will be posted on the PBIS Bulletin Board
- Student will earn VIP access to PBIS celebration

Students earn school-wide celebrations when they consistently show PRIDE as an entire school. Celebrations will take place approximately every nine weeks. Celebrations will be tied to a school-wide goal. For example, if the amount of discipline referrals seems to be an area of concern (based on data collected by the staff), students can earn a celebration if they reduce the number of discipline referrals over a nine week period.

Dog Sweeps Announced

Monday, December 10, 2012

Greetings Students,

<u>We will have a school-wide sweep prior to the winter holiday break</u>. One of our main goals is to maintain safety at Turner Middle School, along with a drug-free environment. We have invited the Douglas County Sheriff K-9 Unit to Turner Middle School. **Usually such sweeps are not announced to students**; however, I want to be SURE that you are aware that such practices are legal and are to be expected from time to time. We want all of our students to remain at Turner Middle School and to make appropriate decisions. Therefore, I am personally alerting you in advance of this sweep. **Future sweeps will be unannounced and randomly selected second semester.** During the sweep we will ask you to place your book bags outside of the classroom while you remain inside the classroom. Sniffing dogs will search all bags, purses, and lockers for any illegal substances.

<u>Although we are confident this is not a major issue at Turner Middle School, we are responsible for your safety.</u> Let's continue to have a fantastic year and make appropriate decisions!!!

Sincerely,

Kwame Carr, Turner Middle School

Principal

Cc: All Parents/Guardians

Write-Up Form for Adults not Doing Their Contracted Job…Use WHENEVER Needed!

Duty and Responsibility Violation Notification

Name: Date:

Please permit me to call to your attention your failure to comply with the following duty and/or responsibility as indicated below:

☐ Failure to post attendance properly or to take attendance

☐ Failure to ☐ notify designated administrator of absence ☐ follow protocol for reporting an absence

☐ Late to school

☐ Failure to submit syllabus or failure to submit on time

☐ Failure to report to assigned duty

☐ Failure to report to hall duty

☐ Failure to submit lost and damaged textbook list

☐ Failure to conduct book check and document lost books

☐ Failure to submit substitute folder

☐ Failure to have a substitute folder (red) on desk with three days of emergency plans

☐ Failure to sign-in/sign-out

☐ Failure to attend conference or assigned PTSA night

☐ Failure to manage students

☐ Failure to attend ☐ faculty ☐ department ☐ team ☐ committee ☐ administrative meeting

☐ Failure to attend required or assigned ☐ district ☐ cluster ☐ vertical team meeting

☐ Failure to return parent phone calls or respond to phone calls in mailbox

☐ Failure to follow emergency procedures

☐ Leaving the classroom unsupervised

☐ Failure to dress appropriately

☐ Failure to submit in-school suspension assignments

☐ Failure to submit requested student assignments to the office

☐ Failure to submit lesson plans ☐ on time

☐ Failure to submit a requested report or document on time

☐ Other

☐ First Notice   ☐ Second Notice   ☐ Final Notice

Please provide your explanation for the deficiency:
_____
_____

Please provide the steps that you will take to correct the deficiency:
_____
_____

☐ Conference Requested   Time   ☐ No

Please give this matter your immediate attention and correct your action immediately.

Thank you for your cooperation.

Administrator: Choose an item.   Sign and return to administrator's mailbox

Grade Level Chair: _____

Signature of recipient: _____   Date: _____

Calling Student Meetings Frequently to Address Discipline Expectations

Please plan to allow students to meet briefly with me on **Tuesday 9/4/12** to reiterate our academic and social expectations for the year.

- I will call **7th grade students first at 8:27**. They will be sent to connections immediately following the meeting.
- I will call **6th grade students second at approximately 8:45**. They will be sent back to class immediately following the meeting.
- I will call **8th grade students third at approximately 9:05**. They will report to second period at the ringing of the bell.

Principle 11 – Interviews

> Teacher Interview Prompts (let them do all the talking)

Please discuss the following items to the best of your ability. **This interview will last approximately 40 minutes.** There are 30 items to discuss, so please use your time wisely.

You have three minutes to review these topics before the interview officially begins.

- Resume' experience relating to the current position you're seeking
- Georgia Certification and qualification for this position
- Standards-based classroom and instruction
- Formative Assessments and Summative Assessments
- Data Utilization in the Classroom
- Backward Design as an Instructional Design
- Common Core Curriculum
- Georgia Performance Standards
- Teacher Collaboration
- Lesson Planning and Lesson Delivery
- Differentiation
- Technology Usage
- Exemplars and Exemplary Models
- Re-Teaching and Remediation
- Response to Intervention (RTI)
- Self-Assessment (by students and teachers)
- Classroom Management and Behavior Management
- Learning Focus Schools
- Parental Contact
- Work Ethic and Meeting Deadlines
- Maximizing Instructional Time
- How you handle Diversity
- Professional Learning
- Your Personal Measure(s) of Success as a Teacher
- Five Year Goal(s)
- References – what would they say about you
- How do you go the extra mile AFTER school hours – what else can you offer
- Your Educational Philosophy
- What do you know about Turner Middle School
- Why do you want to be a part of Turner Middle School

- Is there anything you want to add OR are there any questions for me

Counselor Interview Prompts (let them do all the talking)

<u>Counselor Interview Prompts</u>

You will have 20 minutes to sell yourself and your ability to perform at Turner Middle School. Please discuss the following topics, briefly, allotting an average of 1 minute for each topic.

- Describe why you are the best pick for counselor at Turner Middle School
- Describe your leadership abilities as it relates to a school counselor
- Describe the main role of a counselor
- Describe the counseling theory or approach you most follow; Describe the ASCA National Model
- Describe how you balance your workload and how you stay organized
- Describe how you would handle an irate parent
- Describe how you would handle students with attendance problems
- Describe your greatest asset
- Describe the greatest characteristic of a school counselor
- Summarize what you know about Turner Middle School
- Describe how you handle criticism
- Describe something new you could bring to our program at Turner Middle School
- Describe your work ethic and whether you're willing to work above and beyond school hours to get the job done, giving examples
- Describe your experience with special education students, 504 accommodations, Response to Intervention, and transition plans
- Describe how you deal with cultural differences
- Describe practical experiences you have had that make you feel capable of being a school counselor
- Describe how you resolve conflict between students
- Describe how you would implement small group counseling and classroom guidance
- Describe the counselor's role in standardized testing
- Describe how you handle emergencies, such as child abuse, and confidential situations or information

Administrative Interview Sample Questions

1. What measures will you take to develop, improve and monitor the school budget?
2. Do you believe in a scripted reading program? How would you be sure it's implemented with fidelity?
3. How would you identify teachers having difficulties with instruction and classroom management and how would you assist these teachers with improving instruction and classroom management? What do you look for first when observing a class?
4. Explain initiatives you would implement in regards to Value-Added. What areas would you focus on and why?
5. What is the most difficult decision that you had to make as an administrator that teachers did not necessarily agree with?
6. How will you know when the curriculum is being taught and mastered?
7. How do you maintain morale among your staff?
8. How do you involve all stakeholders and foster positive community relations? How do you go into a school with a set culture after a loved principal leaves?

Principal Interview – Principal Juanita Nelson 2006

Q: Why did you choose leadership?

A: Leadership came natural to me. As a classroom teacher I had a lot of success. My administrators at the time saw qualities in me that had potential and they pushed me in that direction by giving my leadership tasks. I eventually went back to school to obtain my certificate and things unfolded from there. I didn't start out with leadership in mind however. I evolved after several years of teaching.

Q: What are some barriers to leadership (i.e. things that are not so obvious)?

A: Choosing how to budget your money. Budgets require a lot of informed thought when it comes to student achievement. Correctly interpreting needs based upon school data, in regards to budget allocation, becomes critical in all areas of school leadership.

Q: How do you select personnel?

A: I select personnel based upon quality. I have a vision in mind when I hire and then I go about finding that person. Sometimes it's not perfect, sometimes I get more than I bargained for. Everyone wants the best people. Sometimes good references are not as good as your gut feelings about a person.

Q: How does the democratic process work in your building?

A: This year we're focusing on professional learning communities. We are building leaders and participation in decision making school-wide. Our intent is to use the talent of every teacher to their fullest potential within our building, as well as employ community resources to facilitate student achievement. We've expanded our leadership team this year to include representation throughout the building, across content areas, job functions, and grade levels.

Q: **What's been most challenging, people or things (what are some solutions)?**

A: I would say people. The things come with the people. Everyone has their own unique situations. Luckily my staff has fewer than others I've heard about. At least, that is my perception. Everyday is potentially a challenge in regards to people however. It's usually the same ones on either end of the spectrum. You have those that do what they're supposed to do, and those that don't.

Q: **How do you get the community involved?**

A: We employ several parent liaisons due to our diverse population. Spanish and Vietnamese are the primary secondary languages spoken here. These liaisons are charged with implementing ideas to involve the community, especially given the fact that the majority of our students speak Spanish. They are crucial to our success. They also are members of the local community along with our para-pros. Involving the community not only means educating the children, but also employing the adults. This strengthens our bond with the community.

Q: **What is your plan for personal growth?**

A: I am currently investigating a doctoral program of study in leadership. I want to learn everything I can to help me become more effective. Our school is changing. I really need to understand what has to be done to continue the success we've had thus far. In particular, my ELL population must improve their performance. I plan to make that my research.

Q: **What are you most proud of as a leader?**

A: I'm most proud of student achievement in our school for 6 consecutive years after my arrival. Before my arrival this school was tanking. We straightened it up in a year and continued to improve every year. My first set-back occurred last year because we didn't make AYP. Again, our ELL population didn't pass reading. That accounted for our 24 students who couldn't read English.

Q: How do you handle tough employees?

A: I'm a direct person. I think my teachers and staff know that I'm pretty tough myself. Of course I don't walk around trying to intimidate my staff. I simply meet them where they are and then proceed to raise their level of expectation for themselves.

Q: What have you done to establish yourself as an instructional leader?

A: This year we're implementing professional learning communities. I've always been data driven, so my decisions were always based upon successes and failures in instruction, based upon the data. I engage my staff in conversation and collaboration when students are failing. I ask questions about everything, although my specialty is math. I make sure my teachers can tell me why a student is performing on a particular level. That keeps me involved in instruction. Many times I give advice, outside of regular observations, because I want my staff to continually improve their craft.

Q: Who do you call when you feel like you're in trouble?

A: I call my area superintendent. Not only is she knowledgeable, but she happens to be a great friend of mine. Sometimes I consult other principals in our system or even in other systems. The is not commonplace for me however.

> **Interview with Principal Carr Conducted by Mercer University Student J. Dukes**

J. Dukes
Principal Interview

Reflections of a Successful School Leader

Being an effective school principal is a feat which requires a great deal of mental capacity. It is a very delicate position to hold, due to the impact that a leader's decisions and directions can have on several others and on society. School leadership is believed to be one of the most influential roles one may possess. When studying educational research, several studies reveal the influence that leaders have on school climate, teacher effectiveness, student achievement, teacher retention, community partnerships, etc.

Principals are expected to successfully recruit, retain, and manage people of varied experiences, cultures, ethnicities, political beliefs, teaching styles, and personalities, and somehow facilitate their coming together in an effort to simultaneously pursue a singular school mission and vision. Sustaining a rainbow of individuals on this singular path for 190 days, from year to year, can indeed prove a tedious task; however, it can be accomplished with powerful leadership, proper preparation and training, and with a mental capacity and desire to continuously learning who and what will make your school successful, understand that the "who" and the "what" may change from year to year. Success in leadership mandates a thorough and complete understanding of the needs of the school you lead. In retrospect, Frederick Douglas stated, "A man's greatness consists in his ability to do, in the proper application of his powers, the things needed to be done."

John C. Maxwell, educational expert and scholarly author of *Leadership* 101, declared that one of the attributes of successful leadership is implementing concepts that have made other leaders strong. The Georgia Department of Education acknowledges Kwame Andre Carr as one of Georgia's successful principals, because of his innate ability and skills for making significant gains in a Title I, Focus School. Principal Carr became principal at Turner Middle School in Lithia Springs, GA, during the 2011-2012 school year. Prior to his arrival, the school's reputation was one of low morale, gang activity, and low student achievement. Now, Turner Middle School, known as "The Best Middle School in Georgia," is one of the top performing Title I middle schools in the State of Georgia. Turner Middle School serves the same population of students and also has many of the same teachers who existed when the school faced challenges of poor school climate and culture, as well as low student performance, prior to Principal Carr's arrival. Principal Carr and his staff had the honor of creating a video with Georgia Public Broadcasting sharing best practices and strategies on what made Turner Middle School special and successful.

Aspiring leaders, as well as veteran leaders, continue to seek strategies that will grant them the same success and continuous growth that Principal Carr and Turner Middle School have exemplified and continue to maintain under his leadership. Making effective and professional decisions is one of the duties that principals must practice strategically, adequately, and with assertiveness, on a daily basis. Principal Carr shared insight on his personal leadership experiences on topics such as school budgeting, time management, and human resource requirements. These are the reflections of a successful school leader who proved that change, academic growth, and positive school leadership, specifically in a Title I school, begin with believing in your capabilities.

Principal Carr on School Budgeting

School budgeting is a major responsibility that assistant principals may not encounter until they become principals. Nevertheless, early training and preparation are essential. Principal Carr recalled school budgeting as one of his weaknesses as a first year principal; however, this vital skill is an area of opportunity for several new principals. The overall goal of preparing and administering a school budget is for your school's expenditures to reflect the goals of your school improvement plan. School districts may practice different procedures and protocols on who is responsible for school budgeting and how funds are allocated within the schools. Site-based budgeting places principals in charge of funding all school needs, such as their employee salaries, employee benefits, school supplies, learning manipulatives, etc. Districts that function under this form of budgeting hold principals accountable for administering budgets as large as 5.5 million dollars.

In other districts, appointed county office administrators are responsible for the majority of budgeting needs. County office administrators are responsible for allotting employees equally throughout the school system. This form of budgeting leaves the principal in charge of budgeting the school's basic needs, such as copy machines, copy paper, department chair stipends, and other department needs. Douglas County School System, located in West Georgia, currently operates under this form of budgeting. Principals manage a budget that will begin around $40,000, as opposed to a 5.5 million dollar site-based budget. Principal Carr stated that this form of budgeting is dissolved rather quickly, due to the cost of renting school copy machines and purchasing copy paper. Renting copy machines average around $15,000 yearly, and the paper for these machines may cost approximately $15,000, leaving principals with a budget of only $10,000 to adequately distribute throughout the school. Schools are permitted to enhance the base budget that county office allots by building their own budget through fund-raising. For example, band, chorus, Student Government Association, athletics, and any other departments may host approved fundraisers to aid in the productivity of the school clubs, organizations, and departments hosting the fundraiser.

When planning for the school budget, Principals of Title I schools have even more criteria to adhere to, because Title I schools receive additional revenue in an effort to ensure equal learning opportunities and success for all students. Turner Middle School is a Title I school; therefore, Principal Carr has to carefully itemize expenditures to reflect specific instructional needs of the school and ensure that funds are allocated in a manner that will decrease deficits within academic areas. After desegregating school data in each content area, those areas that exemplify the greatest weakness are where principals should focus on improving. Moreover, principals should prioritize allocating funds of each content area based on the data reflected in the school improvement plan. For example, if the lowest-performing area in your school is Students with Disabilities (SWD) in Science and Social Studies, then principals should primarily consider improving this academic need within their budget. In this case, Principal Carr suggested spending more on hiring SWD teachers in the targeted area, as opposed to spending on "things." His rationale is based on the evidence that smaller class sizes will increase academic student achievement, particularly when an effective teacher is hired. Professional development is also an area that principals should appropriately prepare to allot funding for their faculty and staff. Student preparatory materials, such as practice workbooks which may be utilized to prepare students for statewide assessments, are also included in most schools budgets.

The principal is primarily responsible for about 70% of the school budgeting responsibilities. The school's office manager plays an essential role in ensuring the accuracy of the school's budget, as well as keeping faculty and staff in compliance to the rules and regulations of fundraising, spending, receipting, and depositing school funds. Principal Carr suggest meeting with the office manager frequently to ensure all of these essentials are orchestrated appropriately, and to make sure that the principal remains within the limits of the budgeting plan throughout the school year. The principal may also receive input from assistant principals and department chairs, when planning for school budgeting needs.

Principal Carr on Human Resources

School leaders wear multiple hats. Another essential role that principals must be skilled in is being the human resource facilitator. Principals are responsible for hiring the right people, non-renewing those who are not a good fit for the school, and retaining those who are an asset to the overall success of the school. Principal Carr experienced many challenges upon his arrival at Turner Middle School, as a first year principal. Winning the battle of arriving at a new location as a new principal and change agent took a lot of confidence and positive thinking. Changing the culture and climate of a school is not a simple task, but Principal Carr took the risk of changing many protocols and procedures, based mainly on preconceived notions of how he believed the school needed to run. Initially, the faculty and staff were resistant to change, as many human beings are. As result, several employees submitted transfers. After the staff experienced successes under his leadership, they begin to envision the effectiveness of the changes he had made, and now understood that they were for the overall betterment of the school. Principal Carr disclosed that teachers accept change when they see the positive effect it has on the students and on their careers as well. The Turner Middle School Indians slowly adopted the belief that Turner Middle School IS the best middle school in Georgia. As a result, Principal Carr retained more teachers than he had expected as a first-year principal.

Principal Carr based his formula for teacher retention on learning what his teachers needed. He discovered that most teachers want to feel appreciated, respected, effective, and safe.

They also want a principal who will support them with the management of students. Even though the workload may seem overwhelming at times, recovery comes in knowing that they are making a difference in the lives of children and in the community in which they serve. Teachers and everyone hired yearn for principals to allow them the opportunity to do their job. Faculty and staff members value a school leader who is organized, structured, successful, and runs the school like "a well-oiled machine."

When hiring new teachers, principals should first cover the basics, such as checking proper certification for areas needed, criminal background checks, career history, appropriate references, employment gaps, personal skills and achievements, and life experiences. Experiences are important, because some teachers who lack experience in the environment you lead may not be prepared to be successful at your particular school. For example, hiring a first-year teacher without experience may not be the best fit in a school that faces a lot of academic challenges, teacher turnover, and behavior issues.

Non-renewing a teacher depends on the situation. Principals may non-renew employees based for instructional or non-instructional reasons. The impact of a bad hire affects the climate of the school, as well as many students, particularly if the bad hire is a classroom teacher. Principals may sometimes feel like the "bad guy," but the primary goal of non-renewal is to make the school environment better, especially for students. Principal Carr believes that expediting this process quickly will lower the impact that these hires may have on many students. According to Principal Carr, it is more difficult to non-renew someone who has strong results in the classroom and manages students well, but who may lack the personality or professional skills necessary to get along with their colleagues. Some employees may have issues with duties and responsibilities, which is another reason to consider non-renewal. It is not nearly as challenging to non-renew a teacher who has proven unsuccessful; however, each situation requires proper documentation. When documenting someone for inefficiency and ineffectiveness in the classroom, the teacher is on guard. However, when documenting someone for inefficiency outside of the classroom, the administrator is on guard.

Most counties have guidelines and stipulations on non-renewing a teacher, and these guidelines must be followed extensively. Some districts may require the principal to place the employee on a Professional Development Plan (PDP), which requires multiple observations and continuous documentation. Employees may be written up for not following policies, procedures, and protocols. The employee must acknowledge the write-up, and the Executive Director of Personnel and Policy for the school district must be contacted and knowledgeable of the situations that are occurring with the individual. The principal must also meet with the employee frequently, keeping them up to date of their status. Transparency is pivotal, when non-renewing employees. Communication is critical. Expectations must be clear. This is a challenging task, but it must sometimes be done for the sustainability of your school's mission and vision. It is important to always maintain professionalism and a positive environment during this process.

Principal Carr on Time Management

Time management plays an equally important role in properly managing your campus effectively. Principal Carr utilizes his same philosophy on time management that he practiced as a teacher, instructional Math Coach, assistant principal, and now principal. His philosophy is to never place a timeline on the work that he does, especially since he desires success. The more the workload is shared and absent of a stringent time frame, the more success you will have with managing your time appropriately. Principal Carr explained, "My contract stipulates that I work 230 days of the year as a principal. As a teacher, my contract stipulated that I work 190 days, but

I do not stop working at 230 days, and I didn't stop working at 190 days as a teacher. I don't say I'm done working at 5:00, just because it is the end of a work day, nor do I say I'm done working on Saturday or Sunday." Spreading the workload throughout the 365 days of the year allows him to work more efficiently. It allows him to be more available to teachers and students during regular school hours. It allows him the time to read every email and digest every piece of information relevant to his campus. Principal Carr believes this allows him to act soundly and quickly, rather than being rushed to respond. Though being a principal may sometimes spill over into your personal time with family, Principal Carr feels that it is not that intrusive if you are prepared to take one issue at a time, as it comes, and act on each and every one in a timely manner. Procrastinating and avoiding issues is ineffective. Consistency aligns with effectiveness. Executing plans and protocols also allows you to save time, rather than having to create new plans.

    Principal Carr maintains an open-door policy allowing faculty and staff to speak with him at any time. Allowing interruptions from faculty and staff gives principals the opportunity to address things quickly. As for managing time with parent interruptions, which do occur often, protocols and procedures are in place. Office staff and teachers should be properly trained to adhere to the guidelines in place for parents requesting unscheduled meetings. Principal Carr stated that an issue has to be extremely urgent or "newsworthy" before stopping what he needs to do in order to do what someone else would like him to do. Parents should not be allowed to interrupt teachers or administrators, so as to protect instructional time. Announcements should also be managed properly, to avoid interruptions during the school day.

    Many parents, students, and teachers often feel as if their issue is urgent. It is important to show empathy towards everyone's needs and concerns, but in the grand scheme of things, Principal Carr believes that allowing others to define urgent can take you off task. He relates "urgent" to school safety issues. The safety of students, faculty, and staff is always priority.

When protocols and procedures are in place and consistently implemented appropriately, it preserves time in a school day to meet academic needs and allows issues to be addressed properly. When time is being utilized appropriately, principals are able to be successful. Quick, yet sufficient decision-making is also a great time-management tactic. When principals are managing the facility and organization effectively, most situations that are considered urgent are handled by others in the building before involving the principal.

Principal Carr on Self-Reflection

One of the qualities of a great leader is self-awareness and self-reflection. It allows you to know and understand your personal values, as well as be aware of how it affects your leadership style. Self-reflection allows you to flourish your strengths and it allows you to be open to opportunities for professional development and continuous growth. Principal Carr used this opportunity to share his expertise and experiences on school leadership as a moment to also self-reflect. In closing, Principal Carr noted, "Always keep the highest expectations, always believe in yourself and your abilities, and always listen. Never let those you lead see you sweat. Never complain about your boss, and never contradict yourself without admitting your mistakes."

Principle 12 – Sustaining Initiatives on the Inside and the Outside

Writing Across the Curriculum and Referencing Evidence within Text

From: Kwame Carr
Subject: 5 Writing Days : 2014 - 2015 are 8/20 , 10/22, 12/17, 2/11, 3/18 (Yep!)

Writing Across the Curriculum 5 Day Plan

TIME OF DAY

Writing will occur during the first two scheduled classes immediately following the 8:30 AM bell on the indicated days. Writing will occur in each student's scheduled homeroom until 10:07 AM, i.e. when the bell rings. Please follow all directives outlined by our language arts department and Instructional Lead Teacher, Dr. Lobban. Additional time may be allocated, when needed.

COVERAGE

CONNECTIONS & SPECIAL EDUCATION TEACHERS will rotate and provide relief to 6th, 7th, and/or 8th Grade Homeroom teachers during the writing process, depending upon the day's schedule after the mock assessment. <u>Grade Level Chairs are to design the relief plans, as usual.</u>

WRITING ASSIGNMENTS

Mock Writing Days will incorporate all core content areas, as usual; however, the first two writing days which are designated for ELA and Reading will be the traditional essay with supporting details (five paragraphs), while the remaining writing days for Math, Science, and Social Studies will be shorter responses BUT require students to defend their arguments using evidence cited within provided text. The final three essays will be designed to mimic the **Milestones Assessment** once we're able to ascertain what the assessment actually entails. The 8th Grade Ga. Middle Grades Writing Assessment has been eliminated.

SCHEDULES

Writing Day 1 (August 20 - ELA) : Homeroom, 1st period, 4th period, 3rd period, 6th period, 7th period

Writing Day 2 **(October 22 - Reading)** : Homeroom, 2nd period, 4th period, 5th period, 6th period, 7th period

Writing Day 3 **(December 17 - Math)** : Homeroom, 1st period, 4th period, 3rd period, 6th period, 7th period

Writing Day 4 **(February 11 - Science)** : Homeroom, 4th period (this is a **1/2 day early release**)

Writing Day 5 **(March 18 - Social Studies)** : Homeroom, 2nd period, 4th period, 5th period, 6th period, 7th period

Directions for Writing - sample

From: Carol
Subject: Today's Writing Exercise

Good afternoon colleagues:

Overall, I think the 1st in our series of mock writing events went well; thank you teachers for all your hard work. As we prepare for the next writing day on October 22, here are a few ways in which we can make improvements.

- Homeroom teachers, please ensure that each student has the 3 sheets of loose paper, on his or her desk, properly labeled, and headed prior to Mr. Carr's announcement. This will ensure that writing begins promptly at 8:35.
- Grade level chairs, please ensure that each homeroom teacher is given the required number of prompts based on numbers in each homeroom in a timely manner; this will alleviate teachers having insufficient prompts or no prompts at the last minute.
- Homeroom teachers please have your boards prewritten with the recommended times for each step in the writing process, as well as, follow the verbatim teacher instructions. This will allow students to pace themselves accordingly.
- After the mock assessment, I will collect the writing assignments from all teachers and give them to the Reading Department teachers to assess. The reading teachers will have two months to assess the writings using the writing rubric provided. Please return your completed papers to Mr. Carr on the given due date and make plans to conference with your students once he returns them to you.

More Writing Directions - sample

- This morning you will be doing the mock writing assessment in mathematics.
- Each student should have in his/her possession a math packet.
- If you do not have a packet, please raise your hand and I will give you one.
- Look in your packet and ensure that your math packet consists of 4 questions and ruled paper after each question.
- If you do not have this please raise your hand.
- You may use the two sheets of loose paper if you need more paper. If you do use additional paper, please write your name on each sheet, as well as, the question number.
- This test consists of 4 questions. Some questions have more than one part.
- Please read each question carefully, and then answer the questions that follow. BE SURE TO ANSWER ALL PARTS OF EACH QUESTION.
- You may complete your responses in either pen or pencil.
- You will have 90 minutes to complete this test.
- Please Begin
- At the end of 30 minutes, please say: you have 60 minutes left to complete this test.

- At the end of 60 minutes, please say: you have 30 minutes left to complete this test.
- At the end of 75 minutes, please say: you have 15 minutes left to complete this test.
- At the end of 80 minutes, please say: you have 10 minutes to complete this test.
- At the end of 85 minutes, please say: you have 5 minutes to complete this test.
- At the end of 90 minutes, please say: Please stop writing.

Early Payoffs with Writing Honored at State Capitol

From: Kostoula
Sent: Thursday, November 13, 2014 11:25 AM
Subject: Congratulations! Your Student Won the Middle School Water Essay Contest

Dear Educator,

I'm pleased to inform you that the following students have won the 2014 Middle School Essay Contest.

Jurisdiction	Student Name	School	Grade
Atlanta	Freier	Pace Academy	7
Bartow	Dunn	South Central Middle	6
Cherokee	Sabula	Mill Creek Middle	8
Clayton	Doughty	Rex Mill Middle	7
Cobb	Camp	The Walker School	7
Coweta	Czerwinski	Madras Middle	8
DeKalb	Galloway	Cedar Grove Middle	7
Douglas	Weems	Turner Middle	6
Fayette	Weems	J C Booth Middle	6
Forsyth	Quayle	Piney Grove Middle	8
Fulton	Owens	Fulton Science Academy	6
Gwinnett	Rowe	Couch Middle	7
Hall	Britt	North Hall Middle	7
Henry	Crumbley	Woodland Middle	8
Paulding	Kenney	J A Dobbins Middle	8
Rockdale	Crafts	Memorial Middle	8

Each of these students will receive a $100 cash prize at the December 4th Awards Reception at the Georgia State Capitol. In addition at the reception we will announce the District-wide winner and runner-up.

(FYI – Our student from Turner WON the runner up category – 2nd Place!!!!!)

Career Day Phenomenon by Counselor Dukes

TMS Career Day 2014 Room Assignments

Homeroom -Grade	Guest Speaker(s)	Occupation	Student Escort	Rotate to: (2nd - 3rd Session)
Smith-7th Room 15 (On front sidewalk near flag pole)	(1) Stephanie (2) Douglas & Delmorus (3) Sandra	(1) Farm Bureau (2) Georgia Dept of Agriculture **(Outside Mobile Lab)** (3) Serv Pro	Joshua	2-Marshall 3-London
Marshall-7th Room 13	(1) Jacari & Amber (2) Tiffany	(1) Technology Specialist (2) Cornerstone Chiropractic	Emmanuela	2-London 3-Digsby
London-7th Room 11	(1) Lamont, Eric, Garfield	(1) Top Notch Impressions	Lex	2-Digsby 3-Collins
Digsby-7th Room 10	(1) Gregory (2) Russell (3) Brandon	(1) It's Only Social (2) Community Activist (3) Amirakal Marketing	Nanakofi	2-Collins 3-Matthes
Collins-7th Room 08	(1) John & Ronald (2) Rev. Benjamin	(1) Tuskegee Airman & U.S. Military (2) Cornerstone Baptist Church	Jaylin	2-Mathess 3-Tabue
Mathess-8th Room 07	(1) Martha (2) Chief Chris (3) Starla	(1) 911 Operator/Dispatcher (2) Douglasville Chief of Police (3) State Farm	Grant	2-Tabue 3-Duplessis
Tabue-6th Room 06	(1) Ken (2) Elisha	(1) Lockheed Martin Quality (2) 2013 GA TOTY Finalist, APS	Okojie	2-Duplessis 3-Lobban
Duplessis-8th Room 05	(1) Artist	(1) Eric Thurman	Alexis	2-Lobban 3-Brown
Lobban-8th Room 04	(1) Eric (2) Anslee, Travis, Brian More, Rachel	(1) Magician with a Message (2) CCI-Video & Broadcasting	Jacob	2-Brown 3-Kruzinski

Homeroom-Grade	Guest Speaker(s)	Occupation	Student Escort	Rotate to: (2nd - 3rd Session)
Kruzinski-8th Room 01	(1) Bobby (2) Theresa (3) Valerie	(1) Law Enforcement/Fed. Gov. (2) Dental/Surgical Asst. (3) DC Educator, SMS	Kayleigh	2-Brazil 3-Smalls
Brazil-8th Room 02	(1) Linn (2) Gaye	(1) Safe Kids Cobb & Douglas Health (2) Educator's First	Persia	2-Smalls 3-Boyce
Smalls-7th Room 09	(1) Phillip (2) Ericka	(1) 48 Fitness/Decatur Boxing Club (2) Registered Nurse	Rodolfo	2-Boyce 3-Putman
Boyce-7th Room 12	(1) Sharon (2) Chris	(1) WorkitOut Workshop CPR (2) Aiken Officiating Service	James	2-Putman 3-Smith
Putman-7th Room 14	(1) Monique (2) Rex, Clarissa, Kirsten (3) Corey	(1) Douglas County Solicitor General (2) Tyco (3) Martin, Hall, & Associates	Destiny	2-Smith 3-Marshall
Olorunfemi-6th Room 35	(1) Dr. Barry (2) Brandy	(1) Douglas County Schools (2) Registered Nurse	Kazi	2-Sawatski (Café) 3-Crumbley
Sawatski (Café Stage)-6th	(1) John & the African Drum & Dance Ensemble	(1) Inner Harbour	Kaalyah & Ayanna	2-Crumbley 3-Tumilty (M.C.)
Crumbley-6th Room 23	(1) Arthur (2) Kim	(1) D.J. (2) Professional Counselor	Te'Kiya	2-Tumilty (M.C.) 3-Gilbert
Tumilty-6th Room 24 **(Meet in Media Center)**	(1) Mark (2) Theresa (3) Charlotte	(1) American Taekwon Doe (2) Girls Scouts of Greater Atlanta (3) School Nurse	Tai	2-Gilbert 3-Norred
Gilbert-8th Room 33	(1) Lindsay **(1st Speaker)** (2) John (3) Ashley	(1) American Heart Association (2) Eagle Data Systems (3) Greystone Power PR &	Luis	2-Norred 3-Olorunfemi

Homeroom-Grade	Guest Speaker(s)	Occupation	Student Escort	Rotate to: (2nd - 3rd Session)
Kennedy-6th Room 25	(1) Dana, Dakota, Peter, Amy (2) Ramezia	(1) Gold's Gym (2) Citizen's Trust Bank	Lysa	2-Williams 3-Kidd
Williams-8th Room 27	(1) Margaret (*1st speaker) (2) Darien (Arriving for Session 3) (3) Patricia	(1) PAGE (2) DC Instructional Technology Specialist (3) Wenck Travel Agency	Kaysi	2-Kidd 3-Purcell
Kidd-6th Room 28	(1) Chris (2) Christina (3) Joshua	(1) Sheet Metal Constructor (2) Stevie B's Pizza (3) Publix Supermarket Manager	Mi-Lia	2-Purcell 3-Pitts
Purcell-6th Room 29	(1) Lane (2) Dr. Kris (3) Irving	(1) Kate's Club (2) America's Best (3) Mojoba's Fun Factory	Brianna	2-Pitts 3-Davis
Pitts-6th Room 30	(1) Andrew, Kristi, Jeff, Lauren (2) Lauren	(1) Douglas County District Attorney's Office (2) 2013 Georgia TOTY	Aldo	2-Davis 3-Bulach
Davis-6th Room 31	(1) Thomas (2) Kascia (3) Monique	(1) Firefighter/EMT (2) Beyond the Front Porch (3) Motivational Speaker	Tylon	2-Bulach 3-Kennedy
Bulach-6th Room 32	(1) Gerald (2) Valissa *10:20 (3) Charlotte & Tyrone	(1) Berry Much Yogurt (2) Behavioral Healthcare Specialist (3) Horace Mann Companies	Ruby	2-Kennedy 3-Williams

Presentation Info:

The length of your presentation depends on the number of speakers who are in each session. The list below is the suggested speaking times.

1 Speaker: 45 minutes
2 Speakers: 20-25 minutes
3 Speakers: 15 minutes
4 Speakers: 10 minutes

TMS Career Day 2014 (Teacher Instructions)

Career Day will take place on Friday, May 2, 2014, during 1ˢᵗ -3ʳᵈ periods. Guest speakers will park near the gym. Registration, breakfast, and lunch for guest speakers will take place in the gym. The speakers will report back to the gym when the bell rings for 4th period. Everyone excluding band participants, will report to their **regular 4th period class** and be on normal TMS schedule the rest of the day.

- Please provide instructions for subs if you are going to be out on Friday.

- You will <u>stay with your homeroom class during Career Day</u>. Session 1 is during first period and you will rotate with your homeroom students to your next location when the bell rings for 2ⁿᵈ and 3ʳᵈ period. Your speakers remain in the class. Please DO NOT leave your students with the speakers! There will be 1-4 occupations assigned to each homeroom class. Several guest have confirmed, but we cannot account for no shows. We may need to assign extra guests to the classes or reassign speakers if we have walk-ins arrive on Friday.

- <u>Please make sure your laptops and promethean boards are available and working for the guests before they enter your room for 1ˢᵗ period</u>.

- Connections will be on duty to cover your classes if you have planning during 1-3ʳᵈ periods if you need them.

- Please check attendance for student escorts asap and send them to the gym immediately.

- Encourage the students to dress for success.

- **Please be courteous and leave the front lot available for guest if the gym lot is full.**

- **Provide seats for your speakers**

- If necessary, kindly help monitor speaking time and allow time for Q&A. If your room has. . .
  1 Speaker: 45 minutes
  2 Speakers: 20-25 minutes
  3 Speakers: 15 minutes
  4 Speakers: 10 minutes

- Encourage the students to ask questions, but ensure that they are being respectful to all of our guests.

- You will rotate at the sound of the bell (2ⁿᵈ and 3ʳᵈ periods) to the class near you. A rotation schedule will be provided for you. Some classes may have different locations.

- **Please make sure rooms are clean. Also, respect your colleagues' room when you enter their space. Monitor students and make sure they are leaving the rooms clean.**

Hispanic Heritage Month by Educator K. Brown

From: Katherine Brown
Subject: Hispanic Heritage Month Update

Greetings Turner:

- Today marks the beginning of National Hispanic Heritage Month which extends through October 15th.
- This is also the start of Turner Middle School's exciting month-long celebration of this great culture.
- To kick-off this celebration we have planned daily announcements during each lunch period, and occasionally over the P.A. system that highlight contributions of the Hispanic culture.
- On Friday we will have a Fiesta school dance from 4-6 in the gymnasium; we encourage you to serve as a volunteer for this event.
- The Hispanic Heritage Museum will be erected in the Media Center by Mrs. Gray.
- The Hispanic Country Door judging will commence on this Friday morning. Please be sure to complete your door before leaving school on Thursday.
- Your assigned Hispanic country's name tags have been laminated and will be placed near the door of each fourth period class on today.
- Our culminating event will be our school-wide Hispanic Heritage Month Assembly which will be held on Thursday, October 9th at 8:45 in the gym.

On a final note, the Social Studies Department will host its third collaborative planning session for Hispanic Heritage Month on Thursday September 18th in room 1; we look forward to seeing you there.

EXPECTATIONS / CLASSROOM MANAGEMENT RULES

1. Report to class on time. When entering the classroom, prepare immediately and be seated. Do not stand around the door.

2. Absolutely no eating or drinking in the classroom. Food and beverages are not permitted in the classroom without teacher approval.

3. Keep the classroom neat and clean. Do not leave any item on the floor, under your desk, and do not mark on the desk or walls. Do not throw any items in or across the classroom.

4. Bring your supplies to class daily (notebook, pencil, pen, paper, etc.).

5. All submitted assignments must be neat and legible.

6. Do not use or bother any items or materials that you do not own in the classroom without the teacher's permission.

7. MP3s, tape players, electronic games, iPods, cellular phones, balls, etc. are not permitted to be used in the classroom.

8. Each student is required to complete his or her own work. Any evidence of cheating or copying will result in a grade of zero and will be made up during recreational time.

9. The use of profanity and offensive language and/or disrespectful behavior is unacceptable.

Students who fail to adhere to the aforementioned rules will receive consequences.

Student Signature: _____ **Date:** _____

Parent Signature: _____ **Date:** _____

Principle 13 – Ending the Year Smoothly & With a Bang!

Afterschool Rules for Students

Rule # 1 (and this is the only rule):

If you don't think you should be doing something or you are "sneaking" to do it, then don't do it. You can STILL be suspended from regular school hours for committing any offense that is in violation of Douglas County Schools policy, as indicated on page one of the Douglas County Schools website.

Remember:

- Pay attention to your teacher
- Do your assignments
- No sagging
- Shirts tucked in on young men
- No fighting
- No arguing
- No stealing
- Etc…

Post-Planning Agenda for Teachers - Sample

THURSDAY PM, MAY 30TH

12:30 - 01:30	Lunch on your own (student half day)
01:30 - 03:30	Department – Grade Level Meetings/Work in Rooms
03:30 - 06:00	Building Open

FRIDAY PM, MAY 31ST

12:30 - 01:30	Lunch on your own (student half day)
01:30 - 03:30	Department – Grade Level Meetings/Work in Rooms
03:30 - 06:00	Building Open

MONDAY, JUNE 3RD

08:00 – 9:25	Work in rooms and complete EOY Checklist
09:30 - 11:00	Faculty Meeting (cafeteria) – **DATE CHANGED**
11:00 - 12:00	Lunch – on your own
12:00 – 03:30	Work in rooms and complete EOY Checklist

Teacher Survey Results after My 1st Semester as a Principal 2011 (anonymous survey)

1. How easy is it to get the resources you need to teach at this school?
   - Extremely easy — 8.1%-3
   - Very easy — 40.5%-15
   - Moderately easy — 32.4%-12
   - Slightly easy — 13.5%-5
   - Not at all easy — 5.4%-2

2. How safe do you feel teach at this school?
   - Extremely safe — 54.1%-20
   - Very Safe — 40.5%-15
   - Moderately safe — 5.4%-2
   - Slightly safe — 0%-0
   - Not at all safe — 0%-0

3. How useful is the feedback the principal at this school gives you?
   - Extremely useful — 51.4%-19
   - Very useful — 43.2%-16
   - Moderately useful — 5.4%-2
   - Slightly useful — 0%-0
   - Not at all useful — 0%-0

4. How much support does the administration at this school give to the teaching staff?
   - A great deal — 45.9%-17
   - A lot — 45.9%-17
   - A moderate amount — 8.1%-3
   - A little — 0%-0
   - None at all — 0%-0

5. How reasonable are the expectations for student achievement at this school?
   - Extremely reasonable — 29.7%-11
   - Very reasonable — 35.1%-13
   - Moderately reasonable — 29.7%-11
   - Slightly Reasonable — 5.4%-2
   - Not at all reasonable — 0%-0

6. Does this school give too much attention to standardized tests, too little attention to them, or about the right amount of attention to them?
Much too much	8.1%-3
Somewhat too much	24.3%-9
Slightly too much	5.4%-2
About the right amount	59.5%-22
Slightly too little	2.7%-1
Somewhat too little	0%-0

7. How well do teachers at this school collaborate with each other?
Extremely well	2.7%-1
Very well	45.9%-17
Moderately well	45.9%-17
Slightly well	5.4%-2
Not at all well	0%-0

8. How much attention does this school give to your professional growth?
A great deal	18.9%-7
A lot	32.4%-12
A moderate amount	40.5%-15
A little	8.1%-3
None at all	0%-0

9. Overall, are you satisfied with the teaching experience at this school, neither satisfied nor dissatisfied with it, or dissatisfied with it?
Extremely satisfied	51.4%-19
Moderately satisfied	35.1%-13
Slightly Satisfied	5.4%-2
Neither satisfied nor dissatisfied	5.4%-2
Slightly dissatisfied	2.7%-1
Moderately dissatisfied	0%-0
Extremely dissatisfied	0%-0

10. The first semester is coming to an end. We would like for you to express how the first semester has gone. What are your expectations for the second semester and or improvements to be successful to conclude this school year?

The first semester of this school year has gone well. There have been problems but much has been accomplished. I expect to see much growth in the following weeks and months of the school year. I have started to develop a relationship with the students and have been consistent in having high expectations. I have also been consistent with routine. I believe my efforts this semester and my continued hard work next semester will pay-off with clear results in superior student performance.

The first semester went very well in the classroom and overall.

It is my goal to encourage students to dedicate more time to their studies outside of school hours, so as to add to their own success. I plan to do more to promote learning outside of the classroom.

The first semester has gone very well. I have seen a great improvement in the area of discipline. The students are learning there are consequences for their poor behavior.

The first semester of the school year has gone extremely well. My students along with others feel good and they have expressed how safe they feel as well. My students are constantly adjusting as they visit my classroom. Many complain why we have to do this and that but are getting the job done. Parents have been supportive and there are those who tend to add grief because their student cannot do as they please. Overall, the experience has been great academically. The professional development and the constant meeting drowned me at the beginning, but I found myself in the know of what I was supposed to be doing and knew my expectations.

First semester was tough, challenging, overwhelming, and down-right brutal!!! * Towards the end of the 1st semester, we have settled in to the routine and understand each other better. * 2nd semester will hopefully keep the momentum of a positive learning environment. * 2nd semester would be better if the teachers could have a "real open" forum to air out conflicts. This group is the most divided that I have experienced at TMS and it is sad. We use to all know each other, respect each other's disciplines, and work together. Although there is a great deal of academic collaboration among vertical/horizontal groups, there is 'no unity'. That intrinsic factor is important and permeates into the whole environment..... Kids feel it too.

First semester is almost over. Students are fairly resilient. 2nd semester hopefully we don't lose valuable teaching time due to bad weather. Also need some copy paper.

I think with all of the changes that came this year (CDA's, Administration, structure, etc.), first semester was not bad. I appreciate everyone's tolerance of these changes and I think that many people made efforts to support this much needed progress.

I would like to see teachers show a more respectful attitude towards students and other adults in the building.

I thought things went well, good behavior traits have increased from past years with students. For the most part the students were engaged in their work for me, with the typical exceptions. I just need more hands on materials to get my job done.

Unlike previous years, this has been a wonderful one so far. The support of the administration is great. The new spirit is the one we needed. Kids are kids and adults are adults. Foolishness resides in the heart of every child, the Bible says, and this school understands that teachers are here to help take it out. At last, we can say that what some of these kids don't have at home, they can have it at Turner Middle School. At least there is a strong desire to do just that. Please don't take the foot off the gas. This is the year of the breakthrough.

The semester went well enough. I am a first year teacher, so I reserve my thoughts this time around, as I learn what should and should not be the standard.

The principal has done an excellent job setting, expecting, and demanding high expectations and achievement.

My major concern has to do with communication. I am beginning to feel very paranoid when making a comment or asking a question, addressing administrators and/or collogues. Whenever questions or statements are made, "paper trail" copies are always sent to administrators. Why? Some of these statements or questions don't seem to me to warrant this kind of reaction. It makes me feel like I must constantly be aware of CMA! I don't want to do that! I want to feel that I can work in peace and harmony with everyone here!

The first semester has gone well. We have implemented new programs this year in reading and have installed new technology devices to enhance student learning. Next semester I am looking forward to seeing the results of all the hard work that the teachers and students have put into their learning here at Turner Middle School.

Communication has improved greatly at the school. I think we could have more opportunities for student leadership and student led planning. We really need to learn to utilize the data we have at the school. We do not break down the data and implement things based on the data as much as we should for student achievement.

I anticipate that we as a school will continue to practice our craft to become better educators.

Question (#6) about tests is relative to the school district itself. We have way too many standardized tests for the students and spend more time testing than we need - we should be spending more time teaching.

The level of follow-through of school violations for 7th grade must be enforced by the administration. If this failure continues, the success achieved last year will not be enjoyed this year. Students must be held accountable for disrupting instruction, disobedience and disrespect.

Continue what we are doing. We need to really need to get more parental support. I would like to see them during the day maybe homeroom/lunch. Not just for after school events.

Less focus on paperwork and testing and more focus on students. We need more opportunities to bond with students during school instead of afterschool (ie Games, Tutoring, or Band and Choral Concerts.

I am very pleased with Turner's progress this year and I feel confident that we are moving in the right direction. Two things that frustrate me are - 1) There are several teachers in the building that can be very disrespectful to students at times and I hate to see students belittled by staff members. I also get frustrated knowing that some teachers are not really implementing RTI services correctly.

The first semester has been hard on the teachers, but the semester has gone well.

The first semester has been very successful. The students are doing well with the changes. The administration does a great job in supporting the teachers and making sure everyone follows the same procedures.

Looking forward to WiFi.

2 out of 3 administrators are supportive of the teachers. The refusal to change schedules for any reason is extreme. Sometimes schedules need to be changed for the student's best interest. A schedule should not be set in stone for the convenience of an administrator. Homerooms should not be alphabetical as we may have kids we do not even teach which prevents the formation of complete student/teacher relationships. Other than that the changes to behavior are great. The actual punishment of students for misbehavior is appreciated. The support from the 2 administrators is also reassuring. The math Monday activity does cause students to return to class with out-of-hand behavior so maybe there is a way to modify this activity somehow but I do not have the answer for that issue.

Reiterating Principal Expectations…early on in August!

From: Kwame Carr
Sent: Friday, August 26, 2011 10:50 AM
Subject: Final Tweaking via School-Wide Email

Greetings,

THE OVERWHELMING MAJORITY OF YOU ARE DOING A FANTASTIC JOB!

THANK YOU!!!

For that reason, this will be my <u>**very last**</u> school-wide "reminder" of some particular expectations concerning **adult** behaviors for the remainder of this school year. The few adult violators will be addressed independently, privately, and with proper documentation from me to file, as needed. These behavioral expectations include:

1. Bringing Turner-related issues to me and not to central office personnel - C.O. personnel and I have an agreement to inform me - <u>that was stipulated upon my hiring as principal</u>
2. Monitoring halls during each transition by either being in the doorway or in the hall
3. Using parental contact as your first line of disciplinary defense, outside of extreme situations such as fighting
4. Leaving the cafeteria at your daily designated time of 11:42 or 12:15 or 12:47 depending upon your grade level (yesterday was another "taco day" with 15 minutes to spare)
5. Enforcing dress code among all students on your classroom roster during the time they're under your supervision (<u>no pieces</u> of shirt hanging out on boys...EXCEPT **in** P.E.)
6. Notifying me in advance of all absence requests and <u>calling</u> me by phone, if after hours
7. Signing in daily and on time
8. Teaching and assessing most of the period and not sitting most of the period

These simple expectations will not change and enforcing them will keep our environment and culture conducive to learning!

Olympic Week Tradition – last week of school

6th grade

Monday – Olympics Day

TIME	Session ---Stay with 4th period all day
8:30-8:45	4th period
8:45-11:00	Track – Olympics Connections in charge of events Grade Level teachers in charge of supervision of students.
11:03- 1:00	Lunch
1:00-3:15	Olympics continued in GYM
3:18-3:30	Return to 4th period class for dismissal

Tuesday – EXAM

TIME	Session
8:30-9:45	1st
9:48-11:00	2nd
11:03-1:00	Lunch 4th period
1:03-2:15	6th period
2:18-3:30	7th period

Wednesday –ACTIVITY

TIME	Session – Stay with 4th period all day
8:30-11:00	Gym Time with 4th period
11:03-1:30	Lunch and Movie time in 4th period
1:34-3:15	Outside motivational day 6th grade teachers will supervise
3:15 – 3:30	Return inside to 4th period for dismissal

Thursday 1/2 day

8:30-9:13	2nd
9:16-9:59	5th
10:02-10:45	7th
10:48-12:00	4th

Friday 1/2 day

8:30-9:13	Homeroom
9:16-9:59	Homeroom
10:02-10:45	Homeroom
10:48-12:00	Homeroom

7th grade

Monday – EXAM

TIME	Session
8:30-9:45	3rd
9:48-11:00	5th
11:03-1:00	Lunch 4th period
1:03-2:15	6th period
2:18-3:30	7th period

TUESDAY- ACTIVITY

TIME	Session – Stay with 4th period all day
8:30-11:00	Gym Time with 4th period
11:03-1:30	Lunch and Movie time in 4th period
1:34-3:15	Outside motivational day 6th grade teachers will supervise
3:15 – 3:30	Return inside to 4th period for dismissal

Wednesday– Olympics Day

TIME	Session ---Stay with 4th period all day
8:30-8:45	4th period
8:45-11:00	Track – Olympics Connections in charge of events Grade Level teachers in charge of supervision of students.
11:03- 1:00	Lunch
1:00-3:15	Olympics continued in GYM
3:18-3:30	Return to 4th period class for dismissal

Thursday 1/2 day

8:30-9:13	2nd
9:16-9:59	5th
10:02-10:45	7th
10:48-12:00	4th

Friday 1/2 day

8:30-9:13	Homeroom
9:16-9:59	Homeroom
10:02-10:45	Homeroom
10:48-12:00	Homeroom

8th grade

Monday – ACTIVITY

TIME	Session – Stay with 4th period all day
8:30-11:00	Gym Time with 4th period
11:03-1:30	Lunch and Movie time in 4th period
1:34-3:15	Outside motivational day 6th grade teachers will supervise
3:15 – 3:30	Return inside to 4th period for dismissal

Tuesday – Olympics Day

TIME	Session ---Stay with 4th period all day
8:30-8:45	4th period
8:45-11:00	Track – Olympics Connections in charge of events Grade Level teachers in charge of supervision of students.
11:03- 1:00	Lunch
1:00-3:15	Olympics continued in GYM
3:18-3:30	Return to 4th period class for dismissal

Wednesday – EXAM

TIME	Session
8:30-9:45	1st
9:48-11:00	2nd
11:03-1:00	Lunch 4th period
1:03-2:15	3rd
2:18-3:30	5th

Thursday 1/2 day

8:30-9:13	2nd
9:16-9:59	5th
10:02-10:45	7th
10:48-12:00	4th

Friday 1/2 day

8:30-9:13	Homeroom
9:16-9:59	Homeroom
10:02-10:45	Homeroom
10:48-12:00	Homeroom

Olympic Activities Described in Detail

1. 40 yd. Dash- Students will sprint 40 yards

2. 400 meter run-Students will run 400 meters or 1 lap around the track

3. Long Jump- Students will perform 2 attempts at long jump. The best out of those two will be scored

4. Softball Throw- Each student will have two attempts at throwing a softball as far as they can

5. Wheel Barrow Race- One student will walk with their hands while other student holds their feet. There will be a certain distance to travel

6. Jump Rope Contest- Each class will have 2 turners and 1 jumper. While turners turn the rope, the jumper must jump in and perform as many jumps as possible. You are allowed only one mess up upon entering.

7. Limbo- all participants will start at the same height. Without hands touching the ground or any parts of the body touching the stick you are to go as low as you can.

8. Bench Press- 8th grade only- weight will be continually added to find bench max

9. Sac Race- Students will race to cone while having a pillow case around their legs.

10. Hula Hoop Relay Race- After determining 4th period numbers, each class will be equal. The class will stand in a line holding hands. You must pass the hula hoop down the line without letting go of hands.

11. Obstacle Course- starting on one side of the track, students will go through a set obstacle to the opposite side and back.

12. Push up contest- each student will be given a cup their chest has to come all the way down until the touch the cup for the push up to count.

13. 6 on 6 soccer- one goalie per team. At least 1 female should be in at all times. You can sign up 9 people

14. 5 on 5 basketballs- Each 4th period can have up to 7 students on a team. Only 5 play at a time including a female on the floor at all times. There will be a bracket drawn up for a double elimination tournament.

15. Free Throw Shootout- Students will have one minute to MAKE as many free throws as possible. This will be performed in between the 5 on 5 games.

16. Chess- Students will be sent to library to participate in a chess tournament.

| **End of the Year Checklist Published** |

_____1. A <u>list</u> of all employees, certified and classified, who are not returning for the 2014-2015 school year. The letter of resignation, the Douglas County Termination/Separation form (original to HR; a copy to the employee), and the State of Georgia Department of Labor Separation Notice (original to employee; a copy to HR) should be attached if you have not already submitted this paperwork. Send to HR as soon as you receive a resignation.

_____2. Evaluations for all classified employees in alphabetical order should be sent to HR no later than June 13, 2014.

_____3. Send ID Badges of employees not returning for the 2014-2015 school year. Group these together as terminations. Send to HR no later than June 10, 2014.

_____4. Send ID badges of those transferring to other locations within the county for the 2014-2015 school year. Group these as transfers and indicate new location. Send to HR no later than June 10, 2014.

_____5. A <u>list</u> of all staff members, certified and classified, with their assignments for the 2014-2015 school year. Send to HR no later than June 13, 2014.

_____6. School draft master schedules to area directors by June 13, 2014

_____7. Retention and Placement List for middle and elementary schools by June 4, 2014

_____8. EIP Exit forms for K-5 by June 4, 2014

_____9. Third, fifth and eighth grade Test retake results, envelopes, letters and IEP notices prepared as per directions.

_____10. List of personnel having alarm codes who will not be employed at your school next school year – June 10, 2014

_____11. Summer Emergency Addresses and Telephone Numbers for Principal and Assistant Principal (each school is to turn in 2 addresses/phone numbers) – June 10, 2014

_____12. Special Education teacher checklist (1 per each special education teacher) – No later than June 4, 2014

_____13. Middle and High Schools - Mail report cards through Central Office mailroom (report cards only - no inserts). Call **in advance** to schedule time for one person from each school to assist mailroom personnel with metering report cards.

_____14. School's portion of the student handbook for the next school year (2014-2015) due June 4, 2014 to Area Directors.

_____15. School Council End of the Year Report due June 10, 2014 to Area Directors.

_____16. Email copier meter readings – June 10, 2014 (210 day employees)
June 25, 2014 (240 day employees)

_____17. Equipment inventories – June 9, 2014 – (Annual Property Inventory including technology and cafeteria inventories signed off by the principal, then scanned and e-mailed. Please keep the hard copy with the principal's original signature on file at the school.)

_____18. Collect and store all System issued cell phones and iPads for the summer. Return to staff as they return to work for the next school year. Please ensure that Property Use Agreements are completed as these items are reissued. The Property Use Agreements should be scanned and e-mailed to the Property Control Manager. Please retain all original agreements at the school.

_____19. Laptop Verification Forms – June 9, 2014. Collect and store all System issued laptops from staff that are not 240 days. List laptop Service Tag numbers on the Laptop Verification Form. When staff will retain laptops over the summer, have them sign the equipment out on the Laptop Verification Form and complete a Property Use Agreement. Return laptops to staff as they return to work for the next school year. Please ensure that Property Use Agreements are completed as these computers are reissued. The Laptop Verification Forms should be scanned and e-mailed to the Property Control Manager. Please retain all original agreements at the school.

_____20. Accounts Payable – clear all outstanding purchase orders and invoices by June 6, 2014. Reminder: All FY2014 Travel Reimbursement requests must be submitted to the Finance Office by July 3, 2014.

_____21. School Activity Accounts – End of Year Reminders Checklist e-mailed has been completed which includes reconciling the May 2014 bank statement and submitting any amount due to the Finance Office for outstanding invoices (field trips, professional leave, lost or damaged books, ASP, warehouse supplies, etc.).

_____22. Purchasing Card Documentation – All open PO's Purchase Requests, Receipts, Transaction Logs, Issue Logs, and P-Card Statements – Statement Ending 5/27/2014 by June 4, 2014; Statement Ending 6/27/2014 by June 10, 2014 (210 day employees) July 2, 2014 (240 day employees).

_____23. Submit all payments for Warehouse orders by June 10, 2014.

_____24. Submit a CD for all active and inactive students by June 10, 2014. The CD should include all student records.

_____25. Submit a checklist for all students' permanent record cards by June 10, 2014.

The Last Days of School – Expectations Published

From: Kwame Carr
Sent: Tuesday, May 21, 2013 2:05 PM
To: Turner Middle
Subject: Our Last 7 Days Will Look Much Like This

1. **Wednesday 5/22/13** - Regular Bell Schedule - <u>limit all hall passes all day</u> - no frequent flyers in the hall - no placing students in the hall
2. **Thursday 5/23/13** - Regular Bell Schedule - <u>limit all hall passes all day</u> - no frequent flyers in the hall - no placing students in the hall
3. **Friday 5/24/13** - Olympic Schedule - bells have been requested to be off all day - <u>monitor students as expected</u> - no students will be allowed to roam around freely
4. **Tuesday 5/28/13** - Olympic Schedule - bells have been requested to be off all day - <u>monitor students as expected</u> - no students will be allowed to roam around freely
5. **Wednesday 5/29/13** - Olympic Schedule - bells have been requested to be off all day - <u>monitor students as expected</u> - no students will be allowed to roam around freely
6. **Thursday 5/30/13 - 1/2 day** - <u>Mr. Carr will guide all transitions via PA and reserves the right not to have any transitions other than lunch</u> - **NO hall passes, just like testing**
7. **Friday 5/31/13 - 1/2 day** - <u>Mr. Carr will guide all transitions via PA and reserves the right not to have any transitions other than lunch</u> - **NO hall passes, just like testing**

<u>**Absolute emergencies**</u> are the exception to the expectations above. These expectations will be enforced relentlessly given the blessing of arriving at Turner.

Dress Code for Olympic Days AND 1/2 days (students):

- Shorts are allowed by all; no "short shorts" by anyone
- No tank tops
- No over-the-top exposure of bare skin by anyone
- Shirts <u>do not</u> have to be tucked
- NO SAGGING
- No mini-skirts
- Hats are permitted
- Head bands are permitted
- Bandanas are not permitted
- Pajamas are not permitted

Made in the USA
Columbia, SC
01 October 2021